Spirits in Bondage

ALSO BY C. S. LEWIS

The Pilgrim's Regress
The Problem of Pain
The Screwtape Letters *and* Screwtape Proposes a Toast
Broadcast Talks
The Abolition of Man
Christian Behaviour
Beyond Personality
The Great Divorce
George MacDonald: An Anthology
Miracles
Transposition and Other Addresses
Mere Christianity
Surprised by Joy: The Shape of My Early Life
Reflections on the Psalms
The World's Last Night and Other Essays
The Four Loves
Letters to Malcolm: Chiefly on Prayer
Poems
Of Other Worlds: Essays and Stories
Letters of C. S. Lewis
Narrative Poems
A Mind Awake
On Stories: And Other Essays on Literature
The Business of Heaven: Daily Readings from C. S. Lewis
Present Concerns
All My Road Before Me: The Diary of C. S. Lewis, 1922–1927

For Children

The Lion, the Witch and the Wardrobe
Prince Caspian
The Voyage of the *Dawn Treader*
The Silver Chair
The Horse and His Boy
The Magician's Nephew
The Last Battle

Fiction

Out of the Silent Planet
Perelandra
That Hideous Strength
Till We Have Faces: A Myth Retold
The Dark Tower and Other Stories
Boxen: The Imaginary World of the Young C. S. Lewis

C. S. LEWIS

SPIRITS IN BONDAGE

A Cycle of Lyrics

Edited by Walter Hooper

A Harvest Book
HARCOURT BRACE & COMPANY
San Diego   New York   London

Requests for permission to make copies
of any part of the work should be mailed to:
Permissions Department, Harcourt Brace & Company,
6277 Sea Harbor Drive, Orlando, Florida 32887-6777.

Walter Hooper wishes to thank the Estates of W. H. Lewis and
W. T. Kirkpatrick for permission to quote from their
correspondence with C. S. Lewis and A. J. Lewis; also,
Macmillan Publishing Company for permission to reprint from
*They Stand Together: The Letters of C. S. Lewis to Arthur
Greeves*, edited by Walter Hooper, copyright © 1979 by The
Estate of C. S. Lewis. Excerpts from *Surprised by Joy* © 1955
by C. S. Lewis are reprinted by permission of
Harcourt Brace & Company.

Library of Congress Cataloging-in-Publication Data
Lewis, C. S. (Clive Staples), 1898–1963.
Spirits in bondage.
(A Harvest book)
I. Hooper, Walter. II. Title.
PR6023.E926S6   1983   821'.912   83-132
ISBN 0-15-684748-5 *(pbk.)*

Designed by Ellen LoGiudice

Printed in the United States of America

C D E F G H I J

Contents

PART II: HESITATION

PART III: THE ESCAPE

The land where I shall never be
The love that I shall never see.

Preface

We are all young once. A fact not overlooked by William T. Kirkpatrick, who spent the years 1914–1917 tutoring C. S. Lewis for Oxford. In thanking the twenty-year-old 'Jack' Lewis for a copy of *Spirits in Bondage*, Kirkpatrick took exception to Horace's belief that a young man should wait nine years before publishing the efforts of his youth. In his letter to Jack of April 6, 1919, Kirkpatrick wrote:

> I was about to say I congratulate you. But are we to congratulate the nightingale for being gifted with the power of song? We know it sings because it must. . . . A hardened old critic like Horace may whisper *Nonum prematur in annum.*[1] Good Heavens! Nine years! To youth filled to the brim with emotion, nine years is an eternity. Then let us publish, and even if in after days when we have outgrown that phase we may not look back with unalloyed satisfaction on the first heir of our invention, we may be contented with the thought that men may yet search after it and prize it as a treasure as they have done in the case of Shelley and Tennyson.

Jack Lewis (I use his nickname to distinguish him from his father and brother) did indeed outgrow that phase. And, because he was later to become so famous as an apologist of the Christian Faith, it is enough to speak here of the 'first heir of his invention'. One which, perhaps unknown to his tutor, began in Kirkpatrick's house in Little Bookham, Surrey. Most of my knowledge of the years when these poems were written comes from those eleven (unpublished) typescript volumes of letters, diaries and other papers entitled the 'Lewis Papers: Memoirs of the Lewis Family 1850–1930'. They were edited by Jack's brother, Warren, who in one of his

---

[1]'Suppress for nine years', *Ars Poetica*, 388.

editorial notes mentions that 'In the two years intervening between Easter 1915 and Easter 1917, he wrote fifty-two poems which he copied carefully into an old . . . note book. The whole is entitled "The Metrical Meditations of a Cod" '—'Cod' being 'an expression of humorous and insincere self depreciation'.[2] Because Warren's interest lay principally in the history of the family, he contented himself with such information as this:

> Of the poems included in the 'Metrical Meditations', three are marked as having been written in Easter 1915. Of the three, one was subsequently published, and does not therefore concern us at the moment; of the remaining two we select the following specimen. . . .[3]

'Subsequently published' means that it appeared in *Spirits in Bondage*, and the 'specimen' referred to here is the poem 'The Hills of Down'. There are eight such entries in the 'Lewis Papers'. However, for reasons I cannot understand, Warren accounts for only thirty-three poems from the 'Metrical Meditations'. Probably because he thought the original notebook would survive, he does not provide, except in three instances, the names of the seventeen poems 'subsequently published'. They are 'Noon', from January 1916; 'The Star Bath', from September 1916; and 'Ballade Mystique', from Easter 1917. Unfortunately, it is not only the 'Metrical Meditations' which is lost. Writing to me on March 14, 1968, about the 'Lewis Papers', Warren said, 'Jack himself burnt all documents therein transcribed, including his own diaries, in or soon after 1936.' Fortunately, however, there are eleven 'specimen' poems from the 'Metrical Meditations' which are as yet unpublished and survive in the 'Lewis Papers'.

From another source—Jack's letters to his lifelong friend, Arthur Greeves—we learn of two other poems which found their way into *Spirits in Bondage*. I think 'Milton Read Again (In Surrey)' was written at Mr.

---

[2]'Lewis Papers', vol. IV, p. 306. The letter from Kirkpatrick quoted above is from vol. VI, p. 105. The original of the 'Lewis Papers' is in Wheaton College in Illinois, and there is a copy in the Bodleian Library, Oxford.
[3]*Ibid.*

Kirkpatrick's, because Jack, in his letter to Arthur of March 6, 1917, begins a catalogue of the delights he found in Milton with the words, 'I have finished "Paradise Lost" again, enjoying it more than ever.'[4] Then, in a letter of July 14, 1919, in which he sympathized with Arthur over a little disappointment, he said, 'When I was at Bookham I twice went in for the lyric competition in the Bookman, once with "Night! black Night" and again with the piece which appears as "Ad Astra" in the MS. & "Victory" in the printed book'.[5]

There will be, I imagine, some who will regret that those eleven unpublished poems are not included here. There are reasons. Jack believed that a subtitle—'A Cycle of Lyrics'—was needed to make it clear that what was offered was verse. But there was a more compelling reason if a certain 'plan' was to be realised, a 'plan' that I feared could be frustrated by the addition of other poems. Writing to his father, Albert Lewis, on September 19, 1918, Jack explained:

> The sub-title . . . was not given without a reason: the reason is that the book is not a collection of really independent pieces, but the working out, loosely of course and with digressions, of a general idea. If you can imagine 'In Memoriam' with its various parts in different metres it will give you some idea of the form I have tried to adopt. Such merit as it has depends less on the individual than on the combined effect of the pieces. To call it a cycle is to prepare the reader for this plan and to induce him to follow the order of the poems as I have put them. Probably he will not, but we must do our best. . . . Perhaps you can suggest some simpler and more dignified way of saying that the book is a whole and not a collection.[6]

Jack's father had at this time a typescript of the poems. But from what survives of their correspondence, it seems doubtful if Mr. Lewis understood

---

[4]*They Stand Together: The Letters of C. S. Lewis to Arthur Greeves (1914–1963)*, ed. Walter Hooper (1979), p. 176.
[5]*Ibid.*, p. 255.
[6]'Lewis Papers', vol. VI, p. 37.

the 'general idea' behind the cycle. Because the readers of this second edition of the book are also likely to be confused by at least some of the poems, I think a few facts about the beliefs Jack held at the time are called for.

Those who have read his autobiography, *Surprised by Joy*, may recall that it is an account of how he passed from atheism to Christianity; or, as he says, the story of how his early stabs of 'Joy' or 'inconsolable longing' were interpreted as a desire for one thing after another until, when he became a Christian in 1931, he saw that 'Joy' had all along been a pointer to, and a longing for, God. But 'Joy' was pointing elsewhere when these poems were written. And to best interpret them I go back to the time when the ingredients of these poems began to come together.

Jack became a pupil at Cherbourg House, a preparatory school at Malvern, in 1911. It was there, and primarily because of the influence of the School Matron, who was 'floundering in the mazes of Theosophy, Rosicrucianism, Spiritualism',[7] that the twelve-year-old Jack was drawn towards the occult, at the same time abandoning the Christian revelation. There was a sudden return of 'Joy' in the winter of 1912 when he saw one of Rackham's illustrations for *Siegfried & The Twilight of the Gods*, Margaret Armour's translations of Wagner's librettos. Jack was later to recall that simply upon seeing the name of the book, 'Pure "Northernness" engulfed me: a vision of huge, clear spaces hanging above the Atlantic in the endless twilight of Northern summer, remoteness, severity.'[8] At this time *The Soundbox* was publishing in weekly installments synopses of Wagner's *Ring of the Nibelung*. Without having heard a note of Wagner's operas, and merely from these synopses, Jack wrote 801 lines of an heroic poem.[9]

Later Jack read Margaret Armour's translation of the first two parts of Wagner's *Ring* cycle, *The Rhinegold & The Valkyrie*, as well as whatever other books he could find on Norse mythology. This led to an interest in Celtic and Greek mythology so that by the time he entered Malvern

---

[7]*Surprised by Joy: The Shape of my Early Life* (1955), ch. IV.
[8]*Ibid.*, ch. V.
[9]All 801 lines are preserved in the 'Lewis Papers', vol. III, pp. 321–326.

College in September 1913 the divinities of these mythologies had become the natural furniture of his imagination. What's more, Norse mythology provided him with the substance of a poem entitled 'Loki Bound', into which he was to pour the pessimism of an especially unhappy year (1913–1914) at Malvern. Looking back on it, he wrote in *Surprised by Joy*:

> My Loki . . . was against Odin because Odin had created a world though Loki had clearly warned him that this was a wanton cruelty. Why should creatures have the burden of existence forced on them without their consent? . Loki was a projection of myself; he voiced that sense of priggish superiority whereby I was, unfortunately, beginning to compensate myself for my unhappiness.
>
> The other feature in 'Loki Bound' which may be worth commenting on is the pessimism. I was at this time living, like so many Atheists or Antitheists, in a whirl of contradictions. I maintained that God did not exist. I was also very angry with God for not existing. I was equally angry with Him for creating a world.

During the Easter vacation of 1914 two great pleasures came to Jack. First he learned that, subject to his returning to Malvern for a final term, he would (like Warren before him) go to Mr. Kirkpatrick to be 'crammed' for Oxford. William T. Kirkpatrick, to whom Jack devoted chapter IX of *Surprised by Joy*, had been especially kind to Albert Lewis when he was a student at Lurgan College in Co. Armagh, where Kirkpatrick was Headmaster between the years 1873 and 1899. 'The Great Knock', as Kirkpatrick had been dubbed by the boys of Lurgan College, was now living in semiretirement at 'Gastons', a house in Little Bookham, which adjoins Great Bookham in Surrey. The other pleasure for Jack was the beginning of his friendship with Arthur Greeves, who lived across the road from the Lewises. Arthur lacked Jack's genius, but he knew more about music and painting. By the time they met, Jack had almost completed 'Loki Bound', and during his last term at Malvern and his first at Little Bookham he and Arthur corresponded about the possibility of Arthur setting the poem to music.

Many years later, not realising that this poem would be destroyed with so many other manuscripts, Warren copied extracts of only 119 lines. For those interested in the 'Heroic Pessimism', of which Jack was so enamoured at the time, these lines, in which Loki bewails the 'burden of existence', are a good example:

> Odin! and who art thou to make a soul
> And force it into being? Who art thou
> To bring forth men to suffer in the world
> Without their own desire? Remember this,
> In all the universe the harshest law,
> No soul must ever die: it can but change
> Its form and thro' the myriad years
> Must still drag on for aye its weary course,
> Enduring dreadful things for thy caprice.[10]

Looking back on the lopsided impression he may have given in *Surprised by Joy* of the pessimism which marked his year at Malvern, Jack began chapter VIII thus: 'Reading through what I have just written . . . I find myself exclaiming, "Lies, Lies!" This was really a period of ecstasy. It consisted chiefly of moments when you were too happy to speak, when the gods and heroes rioted through your head. . . . But it does not make the other version a lie. I am telling a story of two lives. They have nothing to do with each other: oil and vinegar, a river running beside a canal, Jekyll and Hyde. Fix your eye on either and it claims to be the sole truth.'

Jack arrived at Little Bookham on September 19, 1914. Albert Lewis and Mr. Kirkpatrick were worried that as the only pupil in that quiet place he would feel isolated and lonely. It turned out to be the reverse. Jack's letters, as well as those of Kirkpatrick, testify to the happiness he was to enjoy for the next three years. Summing it up in chapter IX of *Surprised by Joy*, he said, 'We . . . settled into a routine which has ever since served in my mind

[10]The extracts from 'Loki Bound' are found in the 'Lewis Papers', vol. IV, pp. 218–220.

as an archetype, so that what I still mean when I speak of a "normal" day (and lament that normal days are so rare) is a day of the Bookham pattern.' Kirkpatrick was not one to pass out undeserved bouquets, and in his letter to Albert of October 2, 1914, he gives us an idea of what that pattern was like:

Since Clive came, our reading has been almost exclusively Classical. The ancient Classics are no drudgery to him. On the contrary, they are a source of entertainment and delight. He is one of the rare exceptions among boys, who ought to be learning the Classics. He has not hitherto read much, but what he has read he remembers and can express an opinion about it. At Malvern he had to read whatever they were doing in his form. The Greek was hardly suitable—a dialogue of Plato and the *Bacchae* of Euripides. That he could face it at all was remarkable, for he had never read a line of Xenophon or an easy author. But what was more to be regretted was that he had never touched Homer—an education in himself. I corrected this at once, and we read a book of the *Iliad* in the first week. . . . Classical work occupies us during the day, and in the evening he reads history or literature. He is fond of History, especially if it be of that comprehensive nature, which, instead of burdening the memory with details, introduces the reader to the principles and motives of human action. . . . He is always pleasant, cheerful, and obliging to the highest degree.[11]

And Jack wrote excitedly to his father on October 14, 'We have at last struck the real thing in education, in comfort, in pleasure, and in companions. I could almost believe that Malvern had never existed, or was merely a nightmare which I am glad to forget.'[12]

Meanwhile, Albert had reason to be worried about the safety of his sons. Warren had his training at the Royal Military Academy at Sandhurst cut short by Britain's declaration of war on Germany in August. The next

[11]'Lewis Papers', vol. IV, p. 223.
[12]*Ibid.*, p. 226.

month he was posted to Aldershot in preparation for his being sent to France as a second lieutenant in the Royal Army Service Corps. The very little that Jack said about the war at this time was almost entirely confined to a few letters he wrote to his father, but that little merits attention for the light it sheds on his thoughts about the war while it was going on. It may also help the readers of these poems understand why Jack did not fit as neatly as some would wish into that category advertised in the end-pages of the original edition of *Spirits in Bondage* as a 'Soldier Poet' who wrote 'War Poems'. He had been at Gastons less than a month when many of the papers were forecasting an imminent invasion of Britain by the Germans. 'Possibility' soon turned into 'absolute certainty' in Albert's mind, and he urged Jack to come home. There followed a number of replies from Jack which show that he, too, had been reading about a possible invasion. Even so, he was immune to the panic which gripped his father. After a number of letters in which he tried to subdue that panic, he wrote to him on November 8:

> My dear Papy   . even the four, crisp, dainty postal orders (for which many thanks) cannot deter me from exposing the logical weakness of your position. The arguments, as you will recollect, upon which I based my theory, were briefly as follows: that when evils cannot be averted by him who suffers them, i.e. you and I, who *cannot* go into the army—he would do well to shut his eyes and pretend that they do not exist. For the evil, being in itself a fixed quantity, can neither be multiplied or diminished when it actually descends: but the agony of anticipation may be attenuated to nothing.[13]

By now it ought to be evident that the mythologies, the classics, his vast reading, and his own burgeoning imagination provided Jack with much that has gone into these poems. But still to be noticed is the contribution Kirkpatrick (unconsciously) made to that 'whirl of contradictions' about God more pronounced in these poems than in 'Loki Bound'. Kirkpatrick

[13]*Ibid.*, p. 240.

was already an atheist when Albert first met him, and writing about him in *Surprised by Joy*, Jack said:

> At the time when I knew him, the fuel of Kirk's Atheism was chiefly of the anthropological and pessimistic kind. He was great on *The Golden Bough* and Schopenhauer.
>
> The reader will remember that my own Atheism and Pessimism were fully formed before I went to Bookham. What I got there was merely fresh ammunition for the defence of a position already chosen. Even this I got indirectly from the tone of his mind or independently from reading his books. He never attacked religion in my presence. It is the sort of fact that no one would infer from an outside knowledge of my life, but it is a fact.

I believe Jack meant that his earlier pessimism was to some extent subsumed into that system of thought known as 'pessimism' and which consisted of some well-defined beliefs, many of which were by no means of a lugubrious nature. At least not in the works of Arthur Schopenhauer. This German philosopher, one of Kirkpatrick's favourite authors, is recognised as the classic exponent of pessimism and it is known that he had considerable influence on Richard Wagner and Friedrich Nietzsche. Because Kirkpatrick had only the German edition of Schopenhauer's best-known book, *The World as Will and Idea*, Jack borrowed a translation from the public library. It is in that book that Schopenhauer dismisses God, free-will, and the immortality of the soul as illusions. The supreme Reality —'Will'—which Schopenhauer identifies as the self-consciousness in man, finds its equivalent in the unconscious forces of nature. It is 'Will' that creates the world, even though the world itself is a malignant thing which inveigles us into reproducing and perpetuating life. The way to terminate this malignancy is by asceticism, and primarily chastity, which Schopenhauer believed to be the duty of man. As a stage towards this goal, he believed that a transient place of rest could be found in art, poetry, and, above all, music.

Another author whose books Jack probably borrowed from Kirkpatrick's shelves were those of Nietzsche. It was in *Beyond Good and Evil* that he wrote about his notion of the 'Superman', disciplined and perfected in both mental and physical strength, serene and pitiless, ruthlessly pursuing his path to success, partly by abolishing the values derived from Christianity. However, what irritated Kirkpatrick and was picked up by Jack was the association in some minds of Nietzsche's 'Superman' and Germany's great war machine. It was the blame laid upon Nietzsche in an article, 'The Great Illusion', in *The Times* of September 2, 1914, and its refutation, 'The Nietzschean War', in *The Times Literary Supplement* of October 1 which led Jack to say to his father in a letter of October 14:

> I wonder did you notice the article on Nietzsche in last Sunday's *Times Literary Supplement*, which demonstrates that although we have been told to regard Nietzsche as the indirect author of this war, nothing could be farther removed from the spirit and letter of his teaching? It just shows how we can be duped by an ignorant and loud mouthed cheap press. Kirk, who knows something about N., had anticipated that article with us, and is in high glee at seeing this blunder 'proclaimed on the housetops'.[14]

A little later Jack was writing to his father about a matter which filled him with even greater outrage. It had to do with a man he and the nation had reason to respect. But the 'witch-hunt' was on, as it was to be again in both Britain and the United States during World War II, for those with even the most tenuous relationship to the enemy. Prince Louis of Battenburg, who was born in Austria in 1854 and moved to England when he was a boy, had risen through the ranks of the Royal Navy to become the First Sea Lord. Despite all that Winston Churchill could do, as first lord of the Admiralty, public prejudice forced Prince Louis to resign. Prince Louis, whose family name was changed to Mountbatten in 1917, was the uncle of Lord Mountbatten of Burma and the grandfather of His Royal Highness Prince Philip. In his letter of November 3 Jack said:

[14]*Ibid.*, p. 226.

What do you think of this latest outrage perpetrated by the slander, ignorance, and prejudice of the British nation on those who alone can support it? I mean of course the shameful way in which Prince Louis of Battenburg has been forced to resign. He is, I hear, the only man in the Admiralty who knows his job: he had lived all his life in England: his patriotism, loyalty, and efficiency are admitted by all who have a right to judge. And yet, because a number of ignorant and illiterate clods (who have no better employment than that of abusing their betters) so choose, he must resign. This is what comes of letting a nation be governed by 'the people'. 'Vox populi, vox Diaboli', we might say, reversing an old but foolish proverb.[15]

I do not quote these letters merely for what they tell us about Jack's feelings about Nietzsche and Prince Louis, but to illustrate his fair-mindedness, which is certainly very evident in these poems. Of course he thought the Germans were terrible, but this did not for him excuse the anti-German feelings so rampant in Britain and Ireland. He had—it will be remembered —decided that God (like Odin) was responsible for creating a fallen world. Even so, this did not justify what he describes in 'Satan Speaks' as 'a backward cleaving to the beast' by those around him. I don't know when this poem was written, but in 'Victory', which was written at Bookham, he speaks of 'the barcsark shout of battle' before he took part in the war. ('Baresark', from which we get the word 'berserk', means the 'bear-coats' worn by Norse warriors, who fought with a 'berserker rage'.)

After suggesting that he and his father 'shut their eyes' to the evils of the war, Jack gave up reading newspapers. Still, nothing could check the flow of conversation about the war, and one has to remember that Jack and his father were worried about Warren. Nor could Mr. and Mrs. Kirkpatrick ignore the war, as their son Louis was an officer with the Royal Engineers in Salonika. During July 9–15, 1915, Jack kept a diary, and in the entry for July 19 he recorded: 'Had ghastly dreams about the front and getting wounded last night.'[16] It is impossible to know whether such a dream was

[15]*Ibid.*, p. 240.
[16]*Ibid.*, p. 328.

different from those thousands of other young men may have been having. Still, it might mean that Jack had decided to join up if and when there was reason to do so.

As we have been given such an engaging portrait of Kirkpatrick by Jack, I am probably one of many who would enjoy a portrait of Jack by his tutor. There is something very like one in Kirkpatrick's letters to Albert preserved in the 'Lewis Papers'. Those letters include nothing of what Jack called the 'self-torturing temperament' of the Lewises. Still, for all Kirkpatrick's restraint, they are never dull. Where Jack's quarrel with Malvern ends, Kirkpatrick's picks up. In letter after letter he thunders away at the 'inaccuracies' put into Jack's head by his teachers at Malvern. Indeed, those who find the structure and metres of these poems too formal (I don't) must lay much of the blame upon Kirkpatrick. He insisted upon perfection in every aspect of Jack's work, but he expressed a fatherly concern when he found Jack taking upon himself a heavier intellectual burden than was demanded. Near the end, when Jack was about to go up to Oxford, he mentioned to Albert that whereas he had been his best pupil at Lurgan, so Clive—as he always called him—had been his best pupil *ever*. And as he could never expect to see his likes again he would retire, ending his career on this high note. There is space enough here to give only a sample of some observations he made to Albert about Jack, and they come from volume V of the 'Lewis Papers'. The extracts are from his letters of January 22 and September 16, 1915, and April 7 and September 11, 1916, respectively:

As far as I can judge at present, his tastes and predilections are solely in the direction of books and learning. He has singularly little desire to mingle with mankind, or study human nature. His interests lie in a totally different direction—in the past, in the realm of creative imagination, in the world which the common mind would call unreal, but which is to him the only real one.

He is the most brilliant translator of Greek plays I have ever met. Are we to expect such a soaring Pegasus to get into harness and pull a cart? Something must be conceded to such an unusual literary efflorescence at so early an age. He is *unequal* in his performances.

He has read more classics than any boy I ever had—or indeed I might add than any I ever heard of, unless it be an Addison or Landor or Macaulay. These are people we read of, but I have never met any.

Clive is a problem in his way. Of his native powers there can be no question. His reasoning capacity is beyond his years. But when a man is gifted with so much originality, there is a danger that his actual performance on paper may fail to convey an adequate impression.

The year 1916 was important to Jack in a number of ways which were to affect the tenor and content of his poems. Since February there had been talk about the selection of those to be conscripted. It would appear, however, that Jack had already decided to serve, for in a letter to Arthur of March 7, lamenting the ending of their holidays together, he wrote, 'The days are running in so fast now, and it makes me so sad to think that I shall have only two more sets of holidays of the good old type, for in November comes my 18th birthday, military age, and the "vasty fields" of France, which I have no ambition to face'.[17]

That he could have avoided those 'vasty fields' was made clear when the Military Service Act was published in May 1916. Besides the exemption of those resident in Britain 'for the purpose of their education only', the Act did not apply to citizens of Northern Ireland. Even so, Jack did not want to be exempted, and he decided, provided he was accepted by Oxford, to pass into the Army through the University's Officers' Training Corps. He was later to say in *Surprised by Joy:*

I did not much plume myself . . . for deciding to serve, but I did feel that the decision absolved me from taking any further notice of the war. . . . Accordingly I put the war on one side to a degree which

[17] *They Stand Together,* p. 94.

some people will think shameful and some incredible. Others will call it a flight from reality. I maintain that it was rather a treaty with reality, the fixing of a frontier. I said to my country, in effect, 'You shall have me on a certain date, not before. I will die in your wars if need be, but till then I shall live my own life. You may have my body, but not my mind. I will take part in battles but not read about them.'

Jack had all along preferred to confine his correspondence with Arthur to literature. But a few slighting references to Christianity had begun to worry Arthur, who was a Christian. Early in October 1916 Arthur asked him what he believed. The influence of Schopenhauer and the anthropological views of Sir James Frazer's *Golden Bough* are noticeable in Jack's reply of October 12, which is, as far as I know, the first time he committed his beliefs to paper:

You know, I think, that I believe in no religion. There is absolutely no proof for any of them, and from a philosophical standpoint Christianity is not even the best. All religions, that is, all mythologies to give them their proper name are merely man's own invention—Christ as much as Loki. Primitive man found himself surrounded by all sorts of terrible things he didn't understand—thunder, pestilence, snakes etc: what more natural than to suppose that these were animated by evil spirits trying to torture him. These he kept off by cringing to them, singing songs and making sacrifices etc. . . . Thus religion, that is to say mythology grew up. Often, too, great men were regarded as gods after their death—such as Heracles or Odin: thus after the death of a Hebrew philosopher Yeshua (whose name we have corrupted into Jesus) he became regarded as a god, a cult sprang up, which was afterwards connected with the ancient Hebrew Jahweh-worship, and so Christianity came into being—one mythology among many, but the one that we happen to have been brought up in. . . . I must only add that one's views on religious subjects don't make any difference in morals, of course. A good member of society must of course try to be honest, chaste, truthful, kindly etc: these are things we owe to our manhood & dignity and not to any imagined god or gods. . . .

When I last wrote my week-end books were 'Comus' and the Morte Darthur; last week-end, 'Comus' being finished, its place was taken by Shelley's 'Prometheus Unbound' which I got half through. It is an amazing work. I don't know how to describe it to you; it is more wild & out of the world than any poem I ever read, and contains some wonderful descriptions. Shelley had a great genuis, but his carelessness about rhymes, metre, choice of words etc, just prevents him being as good as he might be. . . . However some parts are so splendid that I could forgive him anything.[18]

Jack went on to complete *Prometheus Unbound* at the same time pushing himself harder than ever in preparation for the scholarship examination. He went to Oxford for the first time on December 4, 1916. The examination took place between December 5–9, after which he went home to Belfast. His fears of failure were laid to rest when he learned that he had been elected to a scholarship at University College. But while he was a member of an Oxford *college*, he was not yet a member of Oxford University. For this he had to pass the entrance examination or 'Responsions', to be given on March 20–26, 1917. The frightening thing about Responsions is that they included elementary mathematics, one subject Jack had no head for. It was, therefore, decided that he would return to Bookham in January for further tuition.

Meanwhile, he made the most of his holidays at home. Warren was later to record that 'In the Christmas holidays of 1916 he added another seven poems to his collection; of these, three were afterwards published. It is a little surprising that we hunt in vain in these seven poems for any hint of the impression which a first sight of the beauty of Oxford might have been expected to make on such a sensitive and receptive nature.'[19]

It is impossible to be sure which three of the poems went into this book. Still, I suspect that 'Victory' was one of them. During these holidays Jack

[18]*Ibid.*, pp. 135–136.
[19]'Lewis Papers', vol. V, p. 170.

began a prose version of what was to become the long narrative poem *Dymer* (1926). When this poem was reprinted in 1950 it was with a preface, in which Jack said:

> What I 'found', what simply 'came to me', was the story of a man who, on some mysterious bride, begets a monster: which monster, as soon as it has killed its father, becomes a god. This story arrived, complete, in my mind somewhere about my seventeenth year.

With Shelley's magnificent lines about 'Victory' and the 'Spirit of Man' ringing in Jack's ears, it does not seem fanciful to me that they may have become combined in some way with his monster-become-god idea. In any event, the last stanza of 'Victory' is the first presentation in print of the original idea behind *Dymer*. The most recent reprint of *Dymer* can be found in Jack's *Narrative Poems* (1969), and those who read the editor's preface will see that the development of *Dymer* from 1916 through 1918 proceeds along a course of thought very similar to that of many of these poems.

In a letter to Arthur of February 20, 1917, Jack mentioned the lines chosen as an epigraph for the title page of *Spirits in Bondage:*

> The land where I shall never be
> The love that I shall never see.

He could not recall where they came from, except that they were quoted somewhere by Andrew Lang. That 'somewhere' was Lang's *History of English Literature*, which Jack read in 1915. The actual lines are 'The love whom I shall never meet, / The land where I shall never be,' and although Lang doesn't say so in his *History*, they came from his own pen.

Following what he remembered as his happiest term at Little Bookham, Jack went up to Oxford to sit for Responsions. And there he was 'handsomely ploughed' in mathematics. In spite of this, he was told that he could come into residence at the beginning of Trinity Term so that he could be tutored in algebra and take Responsions again. Between his arrival home on March 27 and his return to Oxford on April 26, Warren mentions that 'He was more than usually occupied with his "Metrical Meditations" to which he added no fewer than ten pieces; of these, four were published as then written, two were published in an altered form, and four remained unpublished.'[20] Although it is not clear whether it was in the "Metrical Meditations" or written somewhere else, there is a note in the 'Lewis Papers'[21] in which Warren says, 'We have what I presume to be Clive's considered opinion of his own youth, summarised in his "Ballade Mystique", written at Easter 1917 when he was eighteen years old, and published in his "Spirits in Bondage".' There follows a copy of the poem, which is exactly as it appears in this book.

When Jack arrived in Oxford on Thursday, April 26, 1917, he was given a set of rooms in the Radcliffe Quad of University College. He matriculated on April 28, and he joined the Officers' Training Corps the following Monday. Because his letters to Arthur are so alive with a recital of the pleasures he found there, one might easily imagine that he lived much as the students had before the war. But Jack had never seen Oxford in peace-time. Since the beginning of the war parts of the twenty colleges which made up the University had been in use as hospitals or for billeting cadets. Indeed, Jack was one of only eight or nine students in his college, his time being divided between lessons in algebra and training with the O.T.C. Writing to his father on May 17, he said, 'Our "military duties" are as light as they could be. We have a morning parade from 7 till 7.45, and another from 2 till 4, with occasional evening lectures on map reading and such like subjects.'[22]

Then, on June 7, Jack joined a cadet battalion, which necessitated his moving into Keble College. It was there he shared a room with a lad his own age, Edward Francis Courtenay 'Paddy' Moore. Paddy's mother, Mrs. Janie King Moore, and his sister Maureen had moved down from Bristol to be with him, and so it was quite natural that Paddy should introduce

[20] *Ibid.*, p. 197.
[21] *Ibid.*, vol. XI, pp. 255–256.
[22] *Ibid.*, vol. V, p. 212.

Jack to them. Those who have read Roger Lancelyn Green's and my *C. S. Lewis: A Biography*, and *They Stand Together*, will know that Jack formed an instant and great affection for Mrs. Moore, which eventually was to cause a rift between Jack and his father. For the time being, however, Jack was very content with Paddy and some of the other cadets in Keble.

As already indicated, Warren was surprised that Jack did not mention Oxford in any of the poems written after his first sight of it when he was taking the scholarship examination. But on that visit Jack had seen very little of it. Now he was a member of University College, living in another college, and had got the 'feel' of Oxford; I think it almost certain that the poem about Oxford entitled 'Lullaby' was written during this period. Having filled up his 'Metrical Meditations', he left it at home in the care of Arthur. After that he began writing and fair-copying other poems into another notebook. This, too, was left with Arthur, as he wrote to him on June 3, 1918, after he returned from the war, 'By the way, haven't you got a reddy-brown MS. book of mine containing "Lullaby" and several other of my later poems?'[23]

As far back as December 10, 1915, Kirkpatrick had written to Albert Lewis about his younger son's prospects, saying, 'The fact . . . is that while admirably adapted for excellence and in my opinion probably for distinction in literary studies, he is adapted for nothing else. You may make up your mind on that.'[24] Jack knew he was right and it gave him additional reason for pursuing what had already become his private ambition—to be a poet. He wrote to Arthur from Keble College on June 10, 1917:

I am in a strangely productive mood at present and spend my few moments of spare time in scribbling verse. When my 4 months course in the cadet battalion is at an end, I shall, supposing I get a commission allright, have a 4 weeks leave before joining my regiment. During it I propose to get together all the stuff I have perpetrated and see if any kind publisher would like to take it. After that, if the

[23]*They Stand Together*, p. 220.
[24]'Lewis Papers', vol. V, p. 39.

fates decide to kill me at the front, I shall enjoy a 9 days immortality while friends who know nothing about poetry imagine that I must have been a genius—what usually happens in such cases.[25]

It was about a month later that Jack first became very interested in philosophy. Eager to share this new discovery with Arthur, he wrote to him on July 24, 'This week I have been reading the works of Bishop Berkely, an eighteenth century country man of ours, & philosopher. Published under the title of Principles of Human Knowledge etc in the Everyman. The part I have been reading is 3 dialogues written to prove the existence of God—which he does by dis-proving the existence of matter.'[26] The philosopher he was so excited by is, of course, Bishop George Berkeley, and the two books referred to are *Principles of Human Knowledge* and *Three Dialogues between Hylas and Philonous*. It is mainly these books which have caused the Bishop to be celebrated for his metaphysical doctrine, which was a form of 'Subjective Idealism'. Very briefly, he held that when we affirm material things to be real, we mean no more than that they are perceived by us *solely* because they are objects of the thought of God. The only things that exist in a primary sense are spirits, and material objects exist simply in the sense that they are perceived by spirits.

The month of leave came round and lasted from September 18–October 18. However, instead of going directly home, Jack went with the Moores to their home in Bristol. There he spent three weeks, not arriving in Belfast until October 12. This was to cause Albert much pain. It was while at home that Jack learned that he had been gazetted into the 3rd Somerset Light Infantry, and it was probably then that he entrusted his two notebooks of poems to Arthur. On October 19 he joined his regiment at Crown Hill in Devon. Rumours were going about that his battalion would be sent to Ireland. Suddenly, on November 15, they were ordered to the front, following a 48-hour leave. There was not enough time to go home, and Jack wired his father, asking him to meet him at Mrs. Moore's home. Albert could not

[25]*They Stand Together*, p. 192.
[26]*Ibid.*, p 196.

understand the telegram and so remained in Belfast. He had another chance to visit Jack at Southampton, but, for whatever reason, he did not go and Jack crossed to France on November 17 without seeing him. According to the Army Record, Jack was transferred from the 3rd Battalion (which *did* go to Ireland) to the 1st Battalion on November 20, and he reached the front lines on his nineteenth birthday, November 29, 1917. Years later he was to devote a chapter entitled 'Guns and Good Company' in *Surprised by Joy* to his experiences in France. But a more detailed, if less readable, account of his regiment is Everard Wyrall's *History of the Somerset Light Infantry (Prince Albert's) 1914–1919.*

On December 13 Jack told his father, 'I am at present in billets in a certain rather battered town somewhere behind the lines.'[27] And Wyrall, in his *History,* records that 'For the 1st Somersets December was a quiet month, though the opposing guns made movement uncomfortable in the Monchy sector where the Battalion was located.' The 'Monchy sector', which lies between Calais and St. Omer, contains several villages with names beginning with 'Monchy'. One of them is Monchy-Le-Preux, which name Jack used as a subtitle for his 'French Nocturne'. As he was carrying a notebook with him, this was very likely the first poem to be written in it.

Wyrall records that, while still under fire from the enemy, 'The Battalion moved to Woringhem on 26th. And here, on 31st, Christmas celebrations took place.' Even if Jack did not have time to write the 'Ode for New Year's Day' and 'Apology' during this time of celebrations, it seems likely that he found his inspiration for them at Woringhem. I assume that he put these poems together because they have a common theme, and both are addressed to Despoina. Because Despoina is a Greek word for 'mistress' some readers have wrongly concluded that he had in mind some person he knew. But Despoina means 'mistress' in the sense of 'Lady of the House', and the name is used as a title by several classical writers for various goddesses. Plato is one of those who used Despoina in speaking of Persephone, and I believe, given the context, she is the only goddess Jack could have had in mind.

[27]'Lewis Papers', vol. V, p. 249.

Persephone, the daughter of Zeus, was forced to marry Pluto, god of the underworld. However, at the intervention of her mother, Demeter, she was permitted to spend half of every year on earth and the other half beneath the earth as queen of the underworld. In Greek mythology there was a section of the underworld—Tartarus—which was the abode of evil-doers. But Tartarus did not have the same significance for the ancient Greeks as hell does for Christians. In the first stanza of his 'Apology' Jack explains to Despoina why he cannot 'build a heaven of dreams in *real* hell'.

And this is as good a place as any to mention that the conviction was growing in Jack that nature was evil. In looking for a way of expressing it he recalled Tennyson's line from *In Memoriam*—'Nature, red in tooth and claw'. As will be seen in many of these poems 'red' becomes a synonym for 'cruel'. Thus, 'red wrath', 'red God', and 'red Nature'.

At the beginning of February Jack, as he says in 'Guns and Good Company', 'had the good luck to fall sick with what the troops call "trench fever" and the doctors P.U.O. (Pyrexia, unknown origin)'. He was sent to No. 10 British Red Cross Hospital at Le Tréport, where he was to remain from February 1 to February 28. It was probably there that he wrote and fair-copied some of the poems he composed in France.

By the time he returned to the front, the Bolsheviks were too busy murdering their own people to continue fighting with the allies. The Germans, as a result, withdrew their troops from the Eastern Front and in March they launched their great Spring offensive. By April 3 they were within forty miles of Paris and between April 9–25 they threw everything into the greatest offensive of the war. Jack was wounded on Mount Bernenchon, during the Battle of Arras on April 15, by an English shell which burst behind him. In the Liverpool Merchants Mobile Hospital at Étaples it was discovered that the worst of his wounds were caused by the shrapnel, which entered his left leg and his chest. Although seriously wounded, his letters to Arthur are proof that, while brave in the field, he maintained his independence of mind.

One of the authors he discovered in this hospital was the philosopher John Locke. He seems to have forgotten to tell Arthur that the book he was arguing about was Locke's *Essay Concerning Human Understanding*, in which the author attacks the conception of 'innate ideas'. According to Locke all our ideas come from experience—from sensation or reflection. Pure reality cannot be grasped by the human mind, and consequently there is no sure basis for metaphysics, substance being 'an uncertain supposition of we know not what'. And, as with Berkeley, Jack used Locke's *Essay* for the poetic 'nourishment' he found there.

In a letter to Arthur of May 23, 1918, before he was moved to a hospital in London, he said, 'You will be surprised . . . to hear that my views at present are getting almost monastic about all the lusts of the flesh. They seem to me to extend the domination of matter over us: and, out here, where I see spirit continually dodging matter (shells, bullets, animal fears, animal pains) I have formulated my equation Matter = Nature = Satan. And on the other side Beauty, the only spiritual & non-natural thing I have yet found.'[28] Included in this letter was a copy of his 'Song', in which it will be seen he modifies Locke's notion of 'substances', such as a tree, as being no more than a combination of atoms.

From his bed in Endsleigh Palace Hospital in London, he wrote to Arthur on May 29 explaining (see Locke's *Essay*, Bk. II) that the colour green is not actually in a tree but the result of certain sensations which arise in the brain as a result of the vibration of atoms. 'It follows then', he said,

that neither the tree, nor any material object can be beautiful in itself: I can never see them as they are, and if I could it would give me no delight. The beauty therefore is not in the matter at all, but is something purely spiritual, arising mysteriously out of the relation between me & the tree: or perhaps as I suggest in my Song, out of some indwelling spirit behind the matter of the tree—the Dryad in fact.

You see the conviction is gaining ground on me that after all Spirit does exist; and that we come in contact with the spiritual element by means of these 'thrills'. I fancy that there is Something right outside time & place, which did not create matter, as the Christians

[28]*They Stand Together*, p. 214.

say, but is matter's great enemy: and that Beauty is the call of the spirit in that something to the spirits in us.[29]

In a letter of June 3 he asked Arthur to send him the 'reddy-brown MS. book' containing 'Lullaby' because 'I have decided to copy out all my work of which I approve and get it typed as a step towards possible publishing.' He ended that letter with the assertion that 'I believe in no God . . . but I do believe that I have in me a spirit, a chip, shall we say, of universal spirit; and that, since all good & joyful things are spiritual & non-material, I must be careful not to let matter . . . get too great hold on me, & dull the one spark I have.'[30]

And we must not overlook that 'one spark'. While it is known that some of these poems were recast in order to accommodate new ideas, it ought to be clear that during the years when they were written the spiritual quality of beauty and 'universal Spirit' were as close as the young Lewis came to a belief in God. This was very important to him and, because of this, I draw the reader's attention to those poems in which the importance of these elements find particular expression—'Dungeon Grates', 'Oxford', 'The Roads', and 'Tu Ne Quaesieris' ('Ask not'), which are the opening words of the eleventh of Horace's *Odes*. Jack had for a long time been reading books on psychical research, and the 'lore of Lodge and Myers' mentioned in the first line of this poem is a reference to two well-known men who were at different times president of the Society for Psychical Research. Sir Oliver Joseph Lodge had published in 1916 a very popular book about psychical research called *Raymond*. Frederick W. H. Myers was best known for his *Science and a Future Life*, published in 1893.

Ever since he had been returned to England, Jack had begged his father to visit him. Despite his pleas, Albert Lewis, who was by nature averse to travel, replied that his law firm could not survive his being away just then. Jack was moved to another hospital, Ashton Court, near Bristol on June 25. This was much closer to Belfast, and on September 3 Jack approached

[29]*Ibid.*, p. 217.
[30]*Ibid.*, pp. 220–221.

his father again about a visit, saying, 'Have you not yet decided on a date for coming over? It is four months since I returned from France, and my friends laughingly suggest that "my father in Ireland" of whom they hear is a mythical creation like Mrs. Harris'[31] (the mythical friend of Mrs. Gamp in Charles Dickens's *Martin Chuzzlewit*). Mr. Lewis was hurt by this and Jack apologised. Even so, he remained unvisited. Still, there can be no doubt that Mr. Lewis loved his son, and it gave him immense pleasure to have a share in the planning of this book.

Following a rejection of the book by Macmillans of London in July, it was sent to the firm of William Heinemann. On September 3 the owner of the firm, Mr. William Heinemann, replied that he would be 'pleased' to be its publisher but that he thought it advisable to consider the substitution of other poems for a few which he did not consider on a level with the poet's 'best work'. Accordingly, Jack sent him 'Our Daily Bread', 'The Autumn Morning', 'Alexandrines', 'Tu Ne Quaesieris', and 'Spooks', which replaced five poems in the original typescript.

Immediately after, on September 9, Jack wrote to his father, 'I write in haste to give you a piece of news which I hope will please you not much less than it did me. You are aware that for some years now I have amused myself by writing verses, and a pocket book collection of these followed me through France. Since my return I have occupied myself by revising them, getting them typed with a few additions, and trying to publish them. After a refusal from Macmillans they have, somewhat to my surprise, been accepted by Heinemann. . . . I will send you a copy at once.'[32] Jack broke the news to Arthur in a letter of September 12, in which he mentioned that the book 'is going to be called "Spirits in Prison" by Clive Staples & is mainly strung round the idea that I mentioned to you before—that nature is wholly diabolical & malevolent and that God, if he exists, is outside of and in opposition to the cosmic arrangements'.[33]

The title had been taken from I Peter iii, 19 (Christ 'went and preached

[31]'Lewis Papers', vol. VI, p. 27.
[32]*Ibid*, pp. 30–31.
[33]*They Stand Together*, p. 230.

unto the spirits in prison'.) However, when Jack's father mentioned that Robert Hitchens had published a novel entitled *Spirit in Prison*, he altered the title to *Spirits in Bondage*, borrowed from Milton's *Paradise Lost*. But why, Albert Lewis asked, should he bother with a pseudonym? At this time Jack had no idea how long he would remain in hospital and whether or not, when he was released, he would be sent back to France. 'My only reason', he wrote to his father on September 18, 'for choosing a pseudonym at all was a natural feeling that I should not care to have this bit of my life known in the regiment. One doesn't want either officers or men to talk about "our b——y [bloody] lyrical poet again" whenever I make a mistake."[34] In this same letter he mentioned that his friend Paddy Moore, for a long time missing, was now known to have been killed.

After considering several possible pseudonyms, Jack and his father agreed on 'Clive Hamilton'—Jack's first name and his mother's family name. It was during this discussion that Jack was transferred, on October 4, to Perham Downs Camp at Ludgershall, near Andover. Meanwhile, Mr. Heinemann and his General Manager, Charles Sheldon Evans, were going over the poems very carefully. In a letter of October 8 Mr. Heinemann drew Jack's attention to his too frequent use of the word 'universe', which led not only to some unfortunate rhyming but a tiresomeness caused by the frequency of any particular word. One such example was the rhyming, in the original version of the Prologue, of 'Coracle of verses' to 'brighter universe'.

Jack was able to get up to the offices of William Heinemann on October 25, and there he had the terrifying privilege of meeting Mr. Heinemann and Mr. Evans. After signing the contract, he was told that John Galsworthy had read his manuscript and wished to publish 'Death in Battle' in his newly formed magazine *Reveille*. Jack agreed and his first published poem was to appear in the third (February 1919) number of *Reveille*. Writing to his father on November 10 about this meeting, Jack said, 'We must remember that even when poetry has a "succès fou" it is still less profitable to the publisher than even fairly good fiction. As Evans said to

[34]'Lewis Papers', vol. VI, p. 37

me "We don't expect to make a commercial success out of poetry: we only publish it—well, simply because its good." '[35]

Galsworthy was one of many who considered 'Death in Battle' the most beautiful of the poems. I think there are two reasons why it won so much approval. First, unlike so many who wrote 'war poems,' Jack did not consider war—with its bullets, corpses and barbed-wire—a fit subject for poetry. So, while he did write about the violence and ferocity of war, what he wrote is not gruesome. This in itself makes those poems whose subject is war so peculiarly his own. The other reason has to do with what he was later to call 'Joy'. At this time he had no name for the feelings which mediate this 'intense longing'. He did, however, have the words to describe what he felt. To describe his feelings he drew, as one would expect, from the great reservoir of mythology and the classics. In 'Death in Battle' he turned in particular to the labours of Hercules, one of which was to pluck the golden apples from the Garden of the Hesperides (four nymphs), whose dimly seen island lay at the Westernmost limits of the world. And thus he created what Sir Philip Sidney in his *Defence of Poetry* called a 'speaking picture'.

(With the exception of the name 'Dagda', which Mr. Evans could not identify, none of Jack's readers appeared to have any difficulty with what was then considered part of the common inheritance of mankind. I don't think we can assume so much today, and for this reason I believe some identifications could be helpful. However, rather than annoy learned readers who already know, and unlearned readers who don't want to know, I have confined these definitions to a section of 'Notes'.)

Albert Lewis had read the poems with a very critical eye before he wrote to Warren on September 19, 1918, with obvious pleasure, 'He has done a considerable thing. It is not a common thing for a first book to be published at all. . . . Of course we must not expect too much from it. It may not take the world by storm.   But he has captured the attention of those who should be wise and knowing in such matters.'[36] Warren had

[35]*Ibid.*, p. 65.
[36]*Ibid.*, p. 38.

not seen the poems when he answered his father on September 24, 'Personally I hope it is not too good. What I mean is that a man who writes a brilliant book before he is twenty is likely to go off rather than to improve in later years.'[37]

That Albert and Warren loved Jack dearly is beyond doubt. When the Armistice was signed on November 11 he was the first person in their thoughts. 'Thank God', Warren wrote in his diary that day, 'Jacks has come through it safely, and that nightmare is now lifted from my mind.' And Albert, who for months had been bombarding the War Office with pleas to have his younger son released from the Army, wrote in his diary, 'Armistice signed. War ended. Thanks be to God.'[38]

Jack was busy turning *Dymer* into verse when he was sent to the Officers' Command Depot at Eastbourne in mid-November. From there he wrote to his father lamenting that all the friends he had made as a cadet in Oxford were dead. Worse than any of his wounds, he said, was a recurring nightmare. Then, quite suddenly, he found himself free, and he arrived home on December 27. Warren was already there. They drank champagne.

Jack returned to Oxford on January 13, 1919, to find the evidence of war being gradually removed as the 'demobbed' students returned. He took up residence in his college and embarked on the 'Honour Mods' course in Greek and Latin literature. By this time, Warren had read *Spirits in Bondage* and he expressed his annoyance in a letter to his father of January 28:

While I am in complete agreement with you as to the excellence of parts of [Jack's] book, I am of opinion that it would have been better if it had never been published. . . . Jack's Atheism is I am sure purely academic, but even so, no useful purpose is served by endeavouring to advertise oneself as an Atheist. . . . It is obvious that a profession of a Christian belief is as necessary a part of a man's mental make

[37]*Ibid.*, p. 40.
[38]*Ibid.*, p. 66.

up as a belief in the King, the Regular Army, and the Public Schools.[39]

Mr. Lewis was aware that Jack's dislike of Malvern had for long been a cause of irritation and embarrassment to Warren, who loved the school passionately. He would not take sides against a son who had, with the merest training, emerged from a war seriously wounded but with no complaints. However, when he learned that Warren had taken Jack to task for writing the poems he urged Warren, in a letter of March 9, to remember that, 'He is young and he will learn in time that a man has not absolutely solved the riddle of the heavens above and the earth beneath and the waters under the earth at twenty. I am not going to slop over but I do think that if Oxford does not spoil him . . . he may write something that men would not willingly let die.'[40] His pleasure did 'slop over' a little when *Spirits in Bondage* was published on March 20, 1919, priced 3/6 (about 85 cents). The wartime shortages of almost everything was felt by publishers, and probably no more than 500 copies of the book were printed.

The reading and especially the writing of poetry had been Albert's earliest and greatest love and some of his poems survive in the 'Lewis Papers'. But like so many, he had to put his tedious work—that of a law court solicitor—first. Even so, he was often caricatured in the newspapers of Belfast as an endearing lover of literature. He would have known, and Mr. Kirkpatrick as well, that most young men when they first begin to write poetry are motivated by the urge to unload their feelings, and that poetry is used as the means to that end.

In Jack's case this motive was at least equally balanced, perhaps outweighed, by the urge or the will to learn by practising the craft of poetry as such and for its own sake. Hence the wide variety both of metrical forms and of subject matters through which his disciplined personal feelings were allowed to transpire. He was, then, an apprentice learning his craft. And

[39]*Ibid.*, p. 84.
[40]*Ibid.*, p. 98.

for this reason more concerned, especially in the more 'metaphysical' of these poems, with *how* rather than *what* he was saying.

In predicting that Jack might write something 'that men would not willingly let die' Mr. Lewis was more prophetic than he knew. I am thinking of that footnote in chapter II of Samuel Coleridge's *Biographia Literaria,* in which Coleridge recalls Sir Joshua Reynolds's saying that 'next to the man who formed and elevated the taste of the public, he that corrupted it is commonly the greatest genius'. Those who have read C. S. Lewis's later works must realise that he could have employed his talents as a mighty corrupter. But he didn't. Not even in those poems in which part of him may have been in 'bondage' to the Prince of this World; and if so, it was the mind and not the heart. Those who go on to read his next published book of poetry, *Dymer,* will see that God is not even there conceived of as totally malevolent. And if one goes on through the rest of his *Narrative Poems* to the later *Poems* (1964) one will surely see that both his mind and heart are fully given over to the One who is the greatest poet of all.

We look in vain for a mention of *Spirits in Bondage* in all that Jack published. So, what did he think of this 'first heir of his invention'? It was while I was his private secretary during the last months of his life that the curtain was lifted just a little. Following his retirement from Cambridge in the summer of 1963, he sent me over to retrieve his belongings from Magdalene College. As he had in his library no more than six of the many books he had written, the great surprise of that visit was unlocking his escritoire. There flashed through my mind those words of Howard Carter when he saw for the first time the interior of the tomb of King Tutankhamen. 'Wonderful things', I thought when I saw three copies of *Spirits in Bondage.* Back in Oxford I asked Jack how this could be. 'It was, you know', he said, 'my beginning. Could I help but love my first child?' He most kindly gave me the one copy in mint condition, still in its dust jacket.

It never was my purpose to criticise these poems. Only to bring out of more than half a century's retirement a book which is reprinted exactly as it was in 1919. The scholars will of course say what they like about the poems. Still, I make this small request. As tempting as it may be to think how much better everything could be said in prose, I urge that one at least consider the poems as *poems*. And consider, too, how fortunate we are that Jack didn't take Horace's advice. He knew as well as Mr. Kirkpatrick that after *Nonum prematur in annum* the 'hardened old critic' goes on to say

> What's kept at home you cancel by a stroke:
> What's sent abroad you never can revoke.

Oxford   Walter Hooper
February 17, 1983

PROLOGUE

As of old Phœnician men, to the Tin Isles sailing
Straight against the sunset and the edges of the earth,
Chaunted loud above the storm and the strange sea's
                                                    wailing,
Legends of their people and the land that gave them
                                                    birth—
Sang aloud to Baal-Peor, sang unto the horned
                                                    maiden,
Sang how they should come again with the Brethon
                                                    treasure laden,
Sang of all the pride and glory of their hardy enter-
                                                    prise,
How they found the outer islands, where the unknown
                                                    stars arise;
And the rowers down below, rowing hard as they could
                                                    row,
Toiling at the stroke and feather through the wet and
                                                    weary weather,
Even they forgot their burden in the measure of a
                                                    song,
And the merchants and the masters and the bondmen
                                                    all together,
Dreaming of the wondrous islands, brought the
                                                    gallant ship along;

So in mighty deeps alone on the chainless breezes
                                                    blown

In my coracle of verses I will sing of lands unknown,
Flying from the scarlet city where a Lord that knows
                                                    no pity
Mocks the broken people praying round his iron
                                                  throne,
—Sing about the Hidden Country fresh and full of
                                            quiet green.
Sailing over seas uncharted to a port that none has
                                                    seen.

PART I

The Prison House

SATAN SPEAKS

I AM Nature, the Mighty Mother,
I am the law: ye have none other.

I am the flower and the dewdrop fresh,
I am the lust in your itching flesh.

I am the battle's filth and strain,
I am the widow's empty pain.

I am the sea to smother your breath,
I am the bomb, the falling death.

I am the fact and the crushing reason
To thwart your fantasy's new-born treason.

I am the spider making her net,
I am the beast with jaws blood-wet.

I am a wolf that follows the sun
And I will catch him ere day be done.

II

FRENCH NOCTURNE

(MONCHY-LE-PREUX)

LONG leagues on either hand the trenches spread
And all is still; now even this gross line
Drinks in the frosty silences divine,
The pale, green moon is riding overhead.

The jaws of a sacked village, stark and grim,
Out on the ridge have swallowed up the sun,
And in one angry streak his blood has run
To left and right along the horizon dim.

There comes a buzzing plane: and now, it seems
Flies straight into the moon. Lo! where he steers
Across the pallid globe and surely nears
In that white land some harbour of dear dreams!

False, mocking fancy! Once I too could dream,
Who now can only see with vulgar eye
That he's no nearer to the moon than I
And she's a stone that catches the sun's beam.

What call have I to dream of anything?
I am a wolf. Back to the world again,
And speech of fellow-brutes that once were men
Our throats can bark for slaughter: cannot sing.

THE SATYR

When the flowery hands of spring
Forth their woodland riches fling,
  Through the meadows, through the valleys
Goes the satyr carolling.

From the mountain and the moor,
Forest green and ocean shore
  All the faerie kin he rallies
Making music evermore.

See! the shaggy pelt doth grow
On his twisted shanks below,
  And his dreadful feet are cloven
Though his brow be white as snow—

Though his brow be clear and white
And beneath it fancies bright,
  Wisdom and high thoughts are woven
And the musics of delight,

Though his temples too be fair
Yet two horns are growing there
  Bursting forth to part asunder
All the riches of his hair.

Faerie maidens he may meet
Fly the horns and cloven feet,
    But, his sad brown eyes with wonder
Seeing—stay from their retreat.

VICTORY

ROLAND is dead, Cuchulain's crest is low,
The battered war-gear wastes and turns to rust,
And Helen's eyes and Iseult's lips are dust
And dust the shoulders and the breasts of snow.

The faerie people from our woods are gone,
No Dryads have I found in all our trees.
No Triton blows his horn about our seas
And Arthur sleeps far hence in Avalon.

The ancient songs they wither as the grass
And waste as doth a garment waxen old,
All poets have been fools who thought to mould
A monument more durable than brass.

For these decay: but not for that decays
The yearning, high, rebellious spirit of man
That never rested yet since life began
From striving with red Nature and her ways.

Now in the filth of war, the baresark shout
Of battle, it is vexed. And yet so oft
Out of the deeps, of old, it rose aloft
That they who watch the ages may not doubt.

Though often bruised, oft broken by the rod,
Yet, like the phœnix, from each fiery bed
Higher the stricken spirit lifts its head
And higher—till the beast become a god.

IRISH NOCTURNE

Now the grey mist comes creeping up
From the waste ocean's weedy strand
And fills the valley, as a cup
Is filled of evil drink in a wizard's hand;
And the trees fade out of sight,
Like dreary ghosts unhealthily,
Into the damp, pale night,
Till you almost think that a clearer eye could see
Some shape come up of a demon seeking apart
His meat, as Grendel sought in Harte
The thanes that sat by the wintry log—
Grendel or the shadowy mass
Of Balor, or the man with the face of clay,
The grey, grey walker who used to pass
Over the rock-arch nightly to his prey.
But here at the dumb, slow stream where the willows
                                        hang,
With never a wind to blow the mists apart,
Bitter and bitter it is for thee, O my heart,
Looking upon this land, where poets sang,
Thus with the dreary shroud
Unwholesome, over it spread,
And knowing the fog and the cloud
In her people's heart and head

Even as it lies for ever upon her coasts
Making them dim and dreamy lest her sons should
                                    ever arise
And remember all their boasts;
For I know that the colourless skies
And the blurred horizons breed
Lonely desire and many words and brooding and
                                    never a deed.

SPOOKS

Last night I dreamed that I was come again
Unto the house where my belovèd dwells
After long years of wandering and pain.

And I stood out beneath the drenching rain
And all the street was bare, and black with night,
But in my true love's house was warmth and light.

Yet I could not draw near nor enter in,
And long I wondered if some secret sin
Or old, unhappy anger held me fast;

Till suddenly it came into my head
That I was killed long since and lying dead—
Only a homeless wraith that way had passed.

So thus I found my true love's house again
And stood unseen amid the winter night
And the lamp burned within, a rosy light,
And the wet street was shining in the rain.

APOLOGY

IF men should ask, Despoina, why I tell
Of nothing glad nor noble in my verse
To lighten hearts beneath this present curse
And build a heaven of dreams in real hell,

Go you to them and speak among them thus:
"There were no greater grief than to recall,
Down in the rotting grave where the lithe worms
         crawl,
Green fields above that smiled so sweet to us."

Is it good to tell old tales of Troynovant
Or praises of dead heroes, tried and sage,
Or sing the queens of unforgotten age,
Brynhild and Maeve and virgin Bradamant?

How should I sing of them? Can it be good
To think of glory now, when all is done,
And all our labour underneath the sun
Has brought us this—and not the thing we would?

All these were rosy visions of the night,
The loveliness and wisdom feigned of old.
But now we wake. The East is pale and cold,
No hope is in the dawn, and no delight.

ODE FOR NEW YEAR'S DAY

WOE unto you, ye sons of pain that are this day in
earth,
Now cry for all your torment: now curse your hour
of birth
And the fathers who begat you to a portion nothing
worth.
And Thou, my own belovèd, for as brave as ere thou
art,
Bow down thine head, Despoina, clasp thy pale arms
over it,
Lie low with fast-closed eyelids, clenched teeth,
enduring heart,
For sorrow on sorrow is coming wherein all flesh has
part.
The sky above is sickening, the clouds of God's hate
cover it,
Body and soul shall suffer beyond all word or thought,
Till the pain and noisy terror that these first years
have wrought
Seem but the soft arising and prelude of the storm
That fiercer still and heavier with sharper lightnings
fraught
Shall pour red wrath upon us over a world deform.

Thrice happy, O Despoina, were the men who were
alive

In the great age and the golden age when still the
cycle ran

On upward curve and easily, for then both maid and
man

And beast and tree and spirit in the green earth could
thrive.

But now one age is ending, and God calls home the
stars

And looses the wheel of the ages and sends it spinning
back

Amid the death of nations, and points a downward
track,

And madness is come over us and great and little
wars.

He has not left one valley, one isle of fresh and green

Where old friends could forgather amid the howling
wreck.

It's vainly we are praying. We cannot, cannot check

The Power who slays and puts aside the beauty that
has been.

It's truth they tell, Despoina, none hears the heart's
complaining

For Nature will not pity, nor the red God lend an ear.

Yet I too have been mad in the hour of bitter paining

And lifted up my voice to God, thinking that he
could hear

The curse wherewith I cursed Him because the Good
was dead.

But lo! I am grown wiser, knowing that our own
hearts

Have made a phantom called the Good, while a few
                                        years have sped
Over a little planet. And what should the great
                                        Lord know of it
Who tosses the dust of chaos and gives the suns their
                                        parts?
Hither and thither he moves them; for an hour we
                                        see the show of it:
Only a little hour, and the life of the race is done.
And here he builds a nebula, and there he slays a sun
And works his own fierce pleasure. All things he
                                        shall fulfil,
And O, my poor Despoina, do you think he ever
                                        hears
The wail of hearts he has broken, the sound of human
                                        ill?
He cares not for our virtues, our little hopes and
                                        fears,
And how could it all go on, love, if he knew of laughter
                                        and tears?

Ah, sweet, if a man could cheat him! If you could
                                        flee away
Into some other country beyond the rosy West,
To hide in the deep forests and be for ever at rest
From the rankling hate of God and the outworn
                                        world's decay!

NIGHT

AFTER the fret and failure of this day,
And weariness of thought, O Mother Night,
Come with soft kiss to soothe our care away
And all our little tumults set to right;
Most pitiful of all death's kindred fair,
Riding above us through the curtained air
On thy dusk car, thou scatterest to the earth
Sweet dreams and drowsy charms of tender might
And lovers' dear delight before to-morrow's birth.
Thus art thou wont thy quiet lands to leave
And pillared courts beyond the Milky Way,
Wherein thou tarriest all our solar day
While unsubstantial dreams before thee weave
A foamy dance, and fluttering fancies play
About thy palace in the silver ray
Of some far, moony globe. But when the hour,
The long-expected comes, the ivory gates
Open on noiseless hinge before thy bower
Unbidden, and the jewelled chariot waits
With magic steeds. Thou from the fronting rim
Bending to urge them, whilst thy sea-dark hair
Falls in ambrosial ripples o'er each limb,
With beautiful pale arms, untrammelled, bare
For horsemanship, to those twin chargers fleet
Dost give full rein across the fires that glow
In the wide floor of heaven, from off their feet
Scattering the powdery star-dust as they go.
Come swiftly down the sky, O Lady Night,

Fall through the shadow-country, O most kind,
Shake out thy strands of gentle dreams and light
For chains, wherewith thou still art used to bind
With tenderest love of careful leeches' art
The bruised and weary heart
In slumber blind.

TO SLEEP

I will find out a place for thee, O Sleep—
A hidden wood among the hill-tops green,
Full of soft streams and little winds that creep
    The murmuring boughs between.

A hollow cup above the ocean placed
Where nothing rough, nor loud, nor harsh shall be,
But woodland light and shadow interlaced
    And summer sky and sea.

There in the fragrant twilight I will raise
A secret altar of the rich sea sod,
Whereat to offer sacrifice and praise
    Unto my lonely god:

Due sacrifice of his own drowsy flowers,
The deadening poppies in an ocean shell
Round which through all forgotten days and hours
    The great seas wove their spell.

So may he send me dreams of dear delight
And draughts of cool oblivion, quenching pain,
And sweet, half-wakeful moments in the night
    To hear the falling rain.

And when he meets me at the dusk of day
To call me home for ever, this I ask—
That he may lead me friendly on that way
    And wear no frightful mask.

IN PRISON

I CRIED out for the pain of man,
I cried out for my bitter wrath
Against the hopeless life that ran
For ever in a circling path
From death to death since all began;
Till on a summer night
I lost my way in the pale starlight
And saw our planet, far and small,
Through endless depths of nothing fall
A lonely pin-prick spark of light,
Upon the wide, enfolding night,
With leagues on leagues of stars above it,
And powdered dust of stars below—
Dead things that neither hate nor love it
Nor even their own loveliness can know,
Being but cosmic dust and dead.
And if some tears be shed,
Some evil God have power,
Some crown of sorrows sit
Upon a little world for a little hour—
Who shall remember? Who shall care for it?

DE PROFUNDIS

COME let us curse our Master ere we die,
For all our hopes in endless ruin lie.
The good is dead. Let us curse God most High.

Four thousand years of toil and hope and thought
Wherein men laboured upward and still wrought
New worlds and better, Thou hast made as naught.

We built us joyful cities, strong and fair,
Knowledge we sought and gathered wisdom rare.
And all this time you laughed upon our care,

And suddenly the earth grew black with wrong,
Our hope was crushed and silenced was our song,
The heaven grew loud with weeping. Thou art strong.

Come then and curse the Lord. Over the earth
Gross darkness falls, and evil was our birth
And our few happy days of little worth.

Even if it be not all a dream in vain
—The ancient hope that still will rise again—
Of a just God that cares for earthly pain,

Yet far away beyond our labouring night,
He wanders in the depths of endless light,
Singing alone his musics of delight;

Only the far, spent echo of his song
Our dungeons and deep cells can smite along,
And Thou art nearer. Thou art very strong.

O universal strength, I know it well,
It is but froth of folly to rebel,
For thou art Lord and hast the keys of Hell.

Yet I will not bow down to thee nor love thee,
For looking in my own heart I can prove thee,
And know this frail, bruised being is above thee.

Our love, our hope, our thirsting for the right,
Our mercy and long seeking of the light,
Shall we change these for thy relentless might?

Laugh then and slay. Shatter all things of worth,
Heap torment still on torment for thy mirth—
Thou art not Lord while there are Men on earth.

SATAN SPEAKS

I AM the Lord your God: even he that made
Material things, and all these signs arrayed
Above you and have set beneath the race
Of mankind, who forget their Father's face
And even while they drink my light of day
Dream of some other gods and disobey
My warnings, and despise my holy laws,
Even tho' their sin shall slay them. For which cause,
Dreams dreamed in vain, a never-filled desire
And in close flesh a spiritual fire,
A thirst for good their kind shall not attain,
A backward cleaving to the beast again.
A loathing for the life that I have given,
A haunted, twisted soul for ever riven
Between their will and mine—such lot I give
While still in my despite the vermin live.
They hate my world! Then let that other God
Come from the outer spaces glory-shod,
And from this castle I have built on Night
Steal forth my own thought's children into light,
If such an one there be. But far away
He walks the airy fields of endless day,
And my rebellious sons have called Him long
And vainly called. My order still is strong
And like to me nor second none I know.
Whither the mammoth went this creature too shall go.

THE WITCH

TRAPPED amid the woods with guile
They've led her bound in fetters vile
To death, a deadlier sorceress
Than any born for earth's distress
Since first the winner of the fleece
Bore home the Colchian witch to Greece—
Seven months with snare and gin
They've sought the maid o'erwise within
The forest's labyrinthine shade.
The lonely woodman half afraid
Far off her ragged form has seen
Sauntering down the alleys green,
Or crouched in godless prayer alone
At eve before a Druid stone.
But now the bitter chase is won,
The quarry's caught, her magic's done,
The bishop's brought her strongest spell
To naught with candle, book, and bell;
With holy water splashed upon her,
She goes to burning and dishonour
Too deeply damned to feel her shame,
For, though beneath her hair of flame
Her thoughtful head be lowly bowed
It droops for meditation proud
Impenitent, and pondering yet
Things no memory can forget,

Starry wonders she has seen
Brooding in the wildwood green
With holiness. For who can say
In what strange crew she loved to play,
What demons or what gods of old
Deep mysteries unto her have told
At dead of night in worship bent
At ruined shrines magnificent,
Or how the quivering will she sent
Alone into the great alone
Where all is loved and all is known,
Who now lifts up her maiden eyes
And looks around with soft surprise
Upon the noisy, crowded square,
The city oafs that nod and stare,
The bishop's court that gathers there,
The faggots and the blackened stake
Where sinners die for justice' sake?
Now she is set upon the pile,
The mob grows still a little while,
Till lo! before the eager folk
Up curls a thin, blue line of smoke.
"Alas!" the full-fed burghers cry,
"That evil loveliness must die!"

DUNGEON GRATES

So piteously the lonely soul of man
Shudders before this universal plan,
So grievous is the burden and the pain,
So heavy weighs the long, material chain
From cause to cause, too merciless for hate,
The nightmare march of unrelenting fate,
I think that he must die thereof unless
Ever and again across the dreariness
There came a sudden glimpse of spirit faces,
A fragrant breath to tell of flowery places
And wider oceans, breaking on the shore
For which the hearts of men are always sore.
It lies beyond endeavour; neither prayer
Nor fasting, nor much wisdom winneth there,
Seeing how many prophets and wise men
Have sought for it and still returned again
With hope undone. But only the strange power
Of unsought Beauty in some casual hour
Can build a bridge of light or sound or form
To lead you out of all this strife and storm;
When of some beauty we are grown a part
Till from its very glory's midmost heart
Out leaps a sudden beam of larger light
Into our souls. All things are seen aright

Amid the blinding pillar of its gold,
Seven times more true than what for truth we
hold
In vulgar hours. The miracle is done
And for one little moment we are one
With the eternal stream of loveliness
That flows so calm, aloof from all distress
Yet leaps and lives around us as a fire
Making us faint with overstrong desire
To sport and swim for ever in its deep—
Only a moment.
O! but we shall keep
Our vision still. One moment was enough,
We know we are not made of mortal stuff.
And we can bear all trials that come after,
The hate of men and the fool's loud bestial
laughter
And Nature's rule and cruelties unclean,
For we have seen the Glory—we have seen.

THE PHILOSOPHER

WHO shall be our prophet then,
Chosen from all the sons of men
To lead his fellows on the way
Of hidden knowledge, delving deep
To nameless mysteries that keep
Their secret from the solar day!
Or who shall pierce with surer eye
This shifting veil of bittersweet
And find the real things that lie
Beyond this turmoil, which we greet
With such a wasted wealth of tears?
Who shall cross over for us the bridge of fears
And pass in to the country where the ancient
                              Mothers dwell?

Is it an elder, bent and hoar
Who, where the waste Atlantic swell
On lonely beaches makes its roar,
In his solitary tower
Through the long night hour by hour
Pores on old books with watery eye
When all his youth has passed him by,
And folly is schooled and love is dead
And frozen fancy laid abed,
While in his veins the gradual blood
Slackens to a marish flood?

For he rejoiceth not in the ocean's might,
Neither the sun giveth delight,
Nor the moon by night
Shall call his feet to wander in the haunted
                              forest lawn.
He shall no more rise suddenly in the dawn
When mists are white and the dew lies pearly
Cold and cold on every meadow,
To take his joy of the season early,
The opening flower and the westward shadow,
And scarcely can he dream of laughter and love,
They lie so many leaden years behind.
Such eyes are dim and blind,
And the sad, aching head that nods above
His monstrous books can never know
The secret we would find.
But let our seer be young and kind
And fresh and beautiful of show,
And taken ere the lustyhead
And rapture of his youth be dead,
Ere the gnawing, peasant reason
School him over-deep in treason
To the ancient high estate
Of his fancy's principate,
That he may live a perfect whole,
A mask of the eternal soul,
And cross at last the shadowy bar
To where the ever-living are.

THE OCEAN STRAND

O LEAVE the labouring roadways of the town,
The shifting faces and the changeful hue
Of markets, and broad echoing streets that drown
The heart's own silent music. Though they too
Sing in their proper rhythm, and still delight
The friendly ear that loves warm human kind,
Yet it is good to leave them all behind,
Now when from lily dawn to purple night
Summer is queen,
Summer is queen in all the happy land.
Far, far away among the valleys green
Let us go forth and wander hand in hand
Beyond those solemn hills that we have seen
So often welcome home the falling sun
Into their cloudy peaks when day was done—
Beyond them till we find the ocean strand
And hear the great waves run,
With the waste song whose melodies I'd follow
And weary not for many a summer day,
Born of the vaulted breakers arching hollow
Before they flash and scatter into spray.
On, if we should be weary of their play
Then I would lead you further into land
Where, with their ragged walls, the stately rocks
Shut in smooth courts and paved with quiet sand
To silence dedicate. The sea-god's flocks

Have rested here, and mortal eyes have seen
By great adventure at the dead of noon
A lonely nereid drowsing half a-swoon
Buried beneath her dark and dripping locks.

NOON

Noon! and in the garden bower
The hot air quivers o'er the grass,
The little lake is smooth as glass
And still so heavily the hour
Drags, that scarce the proudest flower
Pressed upon its burning bed
Has strength to lift a languid head:
—Rose and fainting violet
By the water's margin set
Swoon and sink as they were dead
Though their weary leaves be fed
With the foam-drops of the pool
Where it trembles dark and cool,
Wrinkled by the fountain spraying
O'er it. And the honey-bee
Hums his drowsy melody
And wanders in his course a-straying
Through the sweet and tangled glade
With his golden mead o'erladen,
Where beneath the pleasant shade
Of the darkling boughs a maiden
—Milky limb and fiery tress,
All at sweetest random laid—
Slumbers, drunken with the excess
Of the noontide's loveliness.

MILTON READ AGAIN

(IN SURREY)

THREE golden months while summer on us stole
I have read your joyful tale another time,
Breathing more freely in that larger clime
And learning wiselier to deserve the whole.

Your Spirit, Master, has been close at hand
And guided me, still pointing treasures rare,
Thick-sown where I before saw nothing fair
And finding waters in the barren land,

Barren once thought because my eyes were dim.
Like one I am grown to whom the common field
And often-wandered copse one morning yield
New pleasures suddenly; for over him

Falls the weird spirit of unexplained delight,
New mystery in every shady place,
In every whispering tree a nameless grace,
New rapture on the windy seaward height.

So may she come to me, teaching me well
To savour all these sweets that lie to hand
In wood and lane about this pleasant land
Though it be not the land where I would dwell.

SONNET

THE stars come out; the fragrant shadows fall
About a dreaming garden still and sweet,
I hear the unseen bats above me bleat
Among the ghostly moths their hunting call,
And twinkling glow-worms all about me crawl.
Now for a chamber dim, a pillow meet
For slumbers deep as death, a faultless sheet,
Cool, white and smooth. So may I reach the hall
With poppies strewn where sleep that is so dear
With magic sponge can wipe away an hour
Or twelve and make them naught. Why not a year,
Why could a man not loiter in that bower
Until a thousand painless cycles wore,
And then—what if it held him evermore?

THE AUTUMN MORNING

SEE! the pale autumn dawn
Is faint, upon the lawn
   That lies in powdered white
    Of hoar-frost dight.

And now from tree to tree
The ghostly mist we see
   Hung like a silver pall
    To hallow all.

It wreathes the burdened air
So strangely everywhere
   That I could almost fear
    This silence drear

Where no one song-bird sings
And dream that wizard things
   Mighty for hate or love
    Were close above.

White as the fog and fair
Drifting through middle air
   In magic dances dread
    Over my head.

Yet these should know me too
Lover and bondman true,
　　One that has honoured well
　　　The mystic spell

Of earth's most solemn hours
Wherein the ancient powers
　　Of dryad, elf, or faun
　　　Or leprechaun

Oft have their faces shown
To me that walked alone
　　Seashore or haunted fen
　　　Or mountain glen.

Wherefore I will not fear
To walk the woodlands sere
　　Into this autumn day
　　　Far, far away.

PART II

Hesitation

L'APPRENTI SORCIER

SUDDENLY there came to me
The music of a mighty sea
That on a bare and iron shore
Thundered with a deeper roar
Than all the tides that leap and run
With us below the real sun:
Because the place was far away,
Above, beyond our homely day,
Neighbouring close the frozen clime
Where out of all the woods of time,
Amid the frightful seraphim
The fierce, cold eyes of Godhead gleam,
Revolving hate and misery
And wars and famines yet to be.
And in my dream I stood alone
Upon a shelf of weedy stone,
And saw before my shrinking eyes
The dark, enormous breakers rise,
And hover and fall with deafening thunder
Of thwarted foam that echoed under
The ledge, through many a cavern drear,
With hollow sounds of wintry fear.
And through the waters waste and grey,
Thick-strown for many a league away,
Out of the toiling sea arose
Many a face and form of those

Thin, elemental people dear
Who live beyond our heavy sphere.
And all at once from far and near,
They all held out their arms to me,
Crying in their melody,
"Leap in! Leap in, and take thy fill
Of all the cosmic good and ill,
Be as the Living ones that know
Enormous joy, enormous woe,
Pain beyond thought and fiery bliss:
For all thy study hunted this,
On wings of magic to arise,
And wash from off thy filmèd eyes
The cloud of cold mortality,
To find the real life and be
As are the children of the deep!
Be bold and dare the glorious leap,
Or to thy shame, go, slink again
Back to the narrow ways of men."
So all these mocked me as I stood
Striving to wake because I feared the flood.

ALEXANDRINES

THERE is a house that most of all on earth I
hate.
Though I have passed through many sorrows and
have been
In bloody fields, sad seas, and countries desolate,
Yet most I fear that empty house where the grasses
green
Grow in the silent court the gaping flags between,
And down the moss-grown paths and terrace no man
treads
Where the old, old weeds rise deep on the waste
garden beds.
Like eyes of one long dead the empty windows
stare
And I fear to cross the garden, I fear to linger
there,
For in that house I know a little, silent room
Where Someone's always waiting, waiting in the
gloom
To draw me with an evil eye, and hold me fast—
Yet thither doom will drive me and He will win at
last.

IN PRAISE OF SOLID PEOPLE

THANK God that there are solid folk
Who water flowers and roll the lawn,
And sit and sew and talk and smoke,
And snore all through the summer dawn.

Who pass untroubled nights and days
Full-fed and sleepily content,
Rejoicing in each other's praise,
Respectable and innocent.

Who feel the things that all men feel,
And think in well-worn grooves of thought,
Whose honest spirits never reel
Before man's mystery, overwrought.

Yet not unfaithful nor unkind,
With work-day virtues surely staid,
Theirs is the sane and humble mind,
And dull affections undismayed.

O happy people! I have seen
No verse yet written in your praise,
And, truth to tell, the time has been
I would have scorned your easy ways.

But now thro' weariness and strife
I learn your worthiness indeed,
The world is better for such life
As stout, suburban people lead.

Too often have I sat alone
When the wet night falls heavily,
And fretting winds around me moan,
And homeless longing vexes me

For lore that I shall never know,
And visions none can hope to see,
Till brooding works upon me so
A childish fear steals over me.

I look around the empty room,
The clock still ticking in its place,
And all else silent as the tomb,
Till suddenly, I think, a face

Grows from the darkness just beside.
I turn, and lo! it fades away,
And soon another phantom tide
Of shifting dreams begins to play,

And dusky galleys past me sail,
Full freighted on a faerie sea;
I hear the silken merchants hail
Across the ringing waves to me

—Then suddenly, again, the room.
Familiar books about me piled,
And I alone amid the gloom,
By one more mocking dream beguiled.

And still no nearer to the Light,
And still no further from myself,
Alone and lost in clinging night
—(The clock's still ticking on the shelf).

Then do I envy solid folk
Who sit of evenings by the fire,
After their work and doze and smoke,
And are not fretted by desire.

PART III

The Escape

SONG OF THE PILGRIMS

O DWELLERS at the back of the North Wind,
What have we done to you? How have we sinned
Wandering the Earth from Orkney unto Ind?

With many deaths our fellowship is thinned,
Our flesh is withered in the parching wind,
Wandering the earth from Orkney unto Ind.

We have no rest. We cannot turn again
Back to the world and all her fruitless pain,
Having once sought the land where ye remain.

Some say ye are not. But, ah God! we know
That somewhere, somewhere past the Northern snow
Waiting for us the red-rose gardens blow:

—The red-rose and the white-rose gardens blow
In the green Northern land to which we go,
Surely the ways are long and the years are slow.

We have forsaken all things sweet and fair,
We have found nothing worth a moment's care
Because the real flowers are blowing there.

Land of the Lotus fallen from the sun,
Land of the Lake from whence all rivers run,
Land where the hope of all our dreams is won!

Shall we not somewhere see at close of day
The green walls of that country far away,
And hear the music of her fountains play?

So long we have been wandering all this while
By many a perilous sea and drifting isle,
We scarce shall dare to look thereon and smile.

Yea, when we are drawing very near to thee,
And when at last the ivory port we see
Our hearts will faint with mere felicity:

But we shall wake again in gardens bright
Of green and gold for infinite delight,
Sleeping beneath the solemn mountains white,

While from the flowery copses still unseen
Sing out the crooning birds that ne'er have been
Touched by the hand of winter frore and lean;

And ever living queens that grow not old
And poets wise in robes of faerie gold
Whisper a wild, sweet song that first was told

Ere God sat down to make the Milky Way.
And in those gardens we shall sleep and play
For ever and for ever and a day.

Ah, Dwellers at the back of the North Wind,
What have we done to you? How have we sinned,
That ye should hide beyond the Northern wind?

Land of the Lotus, fallen from the Sun,
When shall your hidden, flowery vales be won
And all the travail of our way be done?

Very far we have searched; we have even seen
The Scythian waste that bears no soft nor green,
And near the Hideous Pass our feet have been.

We have heard Syrens singing all night long
Beneath the unknown stars their lonely song
In friendless seas beyond the Pillars strong.

Nor by the dragon-daughter of Hypocras
Nor the vale of the Devil's head we have feared to pass,
Yet is our labour lost and vain, alas!

Scouring the earth from Orkney unto Ind,
Tossed on the seas and withered in the wind,
We seek and seek your land. How have we sinned?

Or is it all a folly of the wise,
Bidding us walk these ways with blinded eyes
While all around us real flowers arise?

But, by the very God, we know, we know
That somewhere still, beyond the Northern snow
Waiting for us the red-rose gardens blow.

SONG

FAERIES must be in the woods
Or the satyrs' laughing broods—
Tritons in the summer sea,
Else how could the dead things be
Half so lovely as they are?
How could wealth of star on star
Dusted o'er the frosty night
Fill thy spirit with delight
And lead thee from this care of thine
Up among the dreams divine,
Were it not that each and all
Of them that walk the heavenly hall
Is in truth a happy isle,
Where eternal meadows smile,
And golden globes of fruit are seen
Twinkling through the orchards green;
Where the Other People go
On the bright sward to and fro?
Atoms dead could never thus
Stir the human heart of us
Unless the beauty that we see
The veil of endless beauty be,
Filled full of spirits that have trod
Far hence along the heavenly sod
And seen the bright footprints of God.

THE ASS

I woke and rose and slipt away
To the heathery hills in the morning grey.

In a field where the dew lay cold and deep
I met an ass, new-roused from sleep

I stroked his nose and I tickled his ears,
And spoke soft words to quiet his fears.

His eyes stared into the eyes of me
And he kissed my hands of his courtesy.

"O big, brown brother out of the waste,
How do thistles for breakfast taste?

"And do you rejoice in the dawn divine
With a heart that is glad no less than mine?

"For, brother, the depth of your gentle eyes
Is strange and mystic as the skies:

"What are the thoughts that grope behind,
Down in the mist of a donkey mind?

"Can it be true, as the wise men tell,
That you are a mask of God as well,

"And, as in us, so in you no less
Speaks the eternal Loveliness,

"And words of the lips that all things know
Among the thoughts of a donkey go?

"However it be, O four-foot brother,
Fair to-day is the earth, our mother.

"God send you peace and delight thereof,
And all green meat of the waste you love,

"And guard you well from violent men
Who'd put you back in the shafts again."

But the ass had far too wise a head
To answer one of the things I said,

So he twitched his fair ears up and down
And turned to nuzzle his shoulder brown.

BALLADE MYSTIQUE

THE big, red house is bare and lone
The stony garden waste and sere
With blight of breezes ocean blown
To pinch the wakening of the year;
My kindly friends with busy cheer
My wretchedness could plainly show.
They tell me I am lonely here—
What do they know? What do they know?

They think that while the gables moan
And casements creak in winter drear
I should be piteously alone
Without the speech of comrades dear;
And friendly for my sake they fear,
It grieves them thinking of me so
While all their happy life is near—
What do they know? What do they know?

That I have seen the Dagda's throne
In sunny lands without a tear
And found a forest all my own
To ward with magic shield and spear,
Where, through the stately towers I rear
For my desire, around me go
Immortal shapes of beauty clear:
They do not know, they do not know.

L'ENVOI

The friends I have without a peer
Beyond the western ocean's glow,
Whither the faerie galleys steer,
They do not know: how should they know?

NIGHT

I KNOW a little Druid wood
Where I would slumber if I could
And have the murmuring of the stream
To mingle with a midnight dream,
And have the holy hazel trees
To play above me in the breeze,
And smell the thorny eglantine;
For there the white owls all night long
In the scented gloom divine
Hear the wild, strange, tuneless song
Of faerie voices, thin and high
As the bat's unearthly cry,
And the measure of their shoon
Dancing, dancing, under the moon,
Until, amid the pale of dawn
The wandering stars begin to swoon. . . .
Ah, leave the world and come away!
The windy folk are in the glade,
And men have seen their revels, laid
In secret on some flowery lawn
Underneath the beechen covers.
Kings of old, I've heard them say,
Here have found them faerie lovers
That charmed them out of life and kissed

Their lips with cold lips unafraid,
And such a spell around them made
That they have passed beyond the mist
And found the Country-under-wave. . . .

Kings of old, whom none could save!

OXFORD

IT is well that there are palaces of peace
And discipline and dreaming and desire,
Lest we forget our heritage and cease
The Spirit's work—to hunger and aspire:

Lest we forget that we were born divine,
Now tangled in red battle's animal net,
Murder the work and lust the anodyne,
Pains of the beast 'gainst bestial solace set.

But this shall never be: to us remains
One city that has nothing of the beast,
That was not built for gross, material gains,
Sharp, wolfish power or empire's glutted feast.

We are not wholly brute. To us remains
A clean, sweet city lulled by ancient streams,
A place of vision and of loosening chains,
A refuge of the elect, a tower of dreams.

She was not builded out of common stone
But out of all men's yearning and all prayer
That she might live, eternally our own,
The Spirit's stronghold—barred against despair.

HYMN (FOR BOYS' VOICES)

ALL the things magicians do
Could be done by me and you
Freely, if we only knew.

Human children every day
Could play at games the faeries play
If they were but shown the way.

Every man a God would be
Laughing through eternity
If as God's his eye could see.

All the wizardries of God—
Slaying matter with a nod,
Charming spirits with his rod,

With the singing of his voice
Making lonely lands rejoice,
Leaving us no will nor choice,

Drawing headlong me and you
As the piping Orpheus drew
Man and beast the mountains through,

By the sweetness of his horn
Calling us from lands forlorn
Nearer to the widening morn—

All that loveliness of power
Could be man's peculiar dower,
Even mine, this very hour;

We should reach the Hidden Land
And grow immortal out of hand,
If we could but understand!

We could revel day and night
In all power and all delight
If we learned to think aright.

XXXII

"OUR DAILY BREAD"

WE need no barbarous words nor solemn spell
To raise the unknown. It lies before our feet;
There have been men who sank down into Hell
    In some suburban street,

And some there are that in their daily walks
Have met archangels fresh from sight of God,
Or watched how in their beans and cabbage-stalks
    Long files of faerie trod.

Often me too the Living voices call
In many a vulgar and habitual place,
I catch a sight of lands beyond the wall,
    I see a strange god's face.

And some day this will work upon me so
I shall arise and leave both friends and home
And over many lands a pilgrim go
    Through alien woods and foam,

Seeking the last steep edges of the earth
Whence I may leap into that gulf of light
Wherein, before my narrowing Self had birth,
    Part of me lived aright

HOW HE SAW ANGUS THE GOD

I HEARD the swallow sing in the eaves and rose
All in a strange delight while others slept,
And down the creaking stair, alone, tip-toes,
    So carefully I crept.

The house was dark with silly blinds yet drawn,
But outside the clean air was filled with light,
And underneath my feet the cold, wet lawn
    With dew was twinkling bright.

The cobwebs hung from every branch and spray
Gleaming with pearly strands of laden thread,
And long and still the morning shadows lay
    Across the meadows spread.

At that pure hour when yet no sound of man,
Stirs in the whiteness of the wakening earth,
Alone through innocent solitudes I ran
    Singing aloud for mirth.

Till I had found the open mountain heath
Yellow with gorse, and rested there and stood
To gaze upon the misty sea beneath,
    Or on the neighbouring wood,

—That little wood of hazel and tall pine
And youngling fir, where oft we have loved to see
The level beams of early morning shine
    Freshly from tree to tree.

Though in the denser wood there's many a pool
Of deep and night-born shadow lingers yet
Where the new-wakened flowers are damp and cool
    And the long grass is wet.

In the sweet heather long I rested there
Looking upon the dappled, early sky,
When suddenly, from out the shining air
    A god came flashing by.

Swift, naked, eager, pitilessly fair,
With a live crown of birds about his head,
Singing and fluttering, and his fiery hair,
    Far out behind him spread,

Streamed like a rippling torch upon the breeze
Of his own glorious swiftness: in the grass
He bruised no feathery stalk, and through the trees
    I saw his whiteness pass.

But, when I followed him beyond the wood,
Lo! he was changed into a solemn bull
That there upon the open pasture stood
    And browsed his lazy full.

THE ROADS

I STAND on the windy uplands among the hills of Down
With all the world spread out beneath, meadow and
sea and town,
And ploughlands on the far-off hills that glow with
friendly brown.

And ever across the rolling land to the far horizon line,
Where the blue hills border the misty west, I see the
white roads twine,
The rare roads and the fair roads that call this heart
of mine.

I see them dip in the valleys and vanish and rise and
bend
From shadowy dell to windswept fell, and still to the
West they wend,
And over the cold blue ridge at last to the great world's
uttermost end.

And the call of the roads is upon me, a desire in my
spirit has grown
To wander forth in the highways, 'twixt earth and
sky alone,
And seek for the lands no foot has trod and the seas
no sail has known:

—For the lands to the west of the evening and east
of the morning's birth,

Where the gods unseen in their valleys green are glad
                    at the ends of earth
And fear no morrow to bring them sorrow, nor night
                    to quench their mirth.

XXXV

HESPERUS

THROUGH the starry hollow
Of the summer night
I would follow, follow
Hesperus the bright,
To seek beyond the western wave
His garden of delight.

Hesperus the fairest
Of all gods that are,
Peace and dreams thou bearest
In thy shadowy car,
And often in my evening walks
I've blessed thee from afar.

Stars without a number,
Dust the noon of night,
Thou the early slumber
And the still delight
Of the gentle twilit hours
Rulest in thy right.

When the pale skies shiver,
Seeing night is done,
Past the ocean-river,

Lightly thou dost run,
To look for pleasant, sleepy lands,
That never fear the sun.

Where, beyond the waters
Of the outer sea,
Thy triple crown of daughters
That guards the golden tree
Sing out across the lonely tide
A welcome home to thee.

And while the old, old dragon
For joy lifts up his head,
They bring thee forth a flagon
Of nectar foaming red,
And underneath the drowsy trees
Of poppies strew thy bed.

Ah! that I could follow
In thy footsteps bright,
Through the starry hollow
Of the summer night,
Sloping down the western ways
To find my heart's delight!

THE STAR BATH

A PLACE uplifted towards the midnight sky
Far, far away among the mountains old,
A treeless waste of rocks and freezing cold,
Where the dead, cheerless moon rode neighbour-
                    ing by—
And in the midst a silent tarn there lay,
A narrow pool, cold as the tide that flows
Where monstrous bergs beyond Varanger stray,
Rising from sunless depths that no man knows;
Thither as clustering fireflies have I seen
At fixèd seasons all the stars come down
To wash in that cold wave their brightness
                    clean
And win the special fire wherewith they crown
The wintry heavens in frost. Even as a flock
Of falling birds, down to the pool they came
I saw them and I heard the icy shock
Of stars engulfed with hissing of faint flame
—Ages ago before the birth of men
Or earliest beast. Yet I was still the same
That now remember, knowing not where or when.

TU NE QUÆSIERIS

For all the lore of Lodge and Myers
I cannot heal my torn desires,
Nor hope for all that man can speer
To make the riddling earth grow clear.
Though it were sure and proven well
That I shall prosper, as they tell,
In fields beneath a different sun
By shores where other oceans run,
When this live body that was I
Lies hidden from the cheerful sky,
Yet what were endless lives to me
If still my narrow self I be
And hope and fail and struggle still,
And break my will against God's will,
To play for stakes of pleasure and pain
And hope and fail and hope again,
Deluded, thwarted, striving elf
That through the window of my self
As through a dark glass scarce can see
A warped and masked reality?
But when this searching thought of mine
Is mingled in the large Divine,
And laughter that was in my mouth
Runs through the breezes of the South,
When glory I have built in dreams
Along some fiery sunset gleams,

And my dead sin and foolishness
Grow one with Nature's whole distress,
To perfect being I shall win,
And where I end will Life begin.

LULLABY

Lullaby! Lullaby!
There's a tower strong and high
Built of oak and brick and stone,
Stands before a wood alone.
The doors are of the oak so brown
As any ale in Oxford town,
The walls are builded warm and thick
Of the old red Roman brick,
The good grey stone is over all
In arch and floor of the tower tall.
And maidens three are living there
All in the upper chamber fair,
Hung with silver, hung with pall,
And stories painted on the wall.
And softly goes the whirring loom
In my ladies' upper room,
For they shall spin both night and day
Until the stars do pass away.
But every night at evèning
The window open wide they fling,
And one of them says a word they know
And out as three white swans they go,

And the murmuring of the woods is drowned
In the soft wings' whirring sound,
As they go flying round, around,
Singing in swans' voices high
A lonely, lovely lullaby.

WORLD'S DESIRE

LOVE, there is a castle built in a country desolate,
On a rock above a forest where the trees are grim and
great,
Blasted with the lightning sharp—giant boulders
strewn between,
And the mountains rise above, and the cold ravine
Echoes to the crushing roar and thunder of a mighty
river
Raging down a cataract. Very tower and forest
quiver
And the grey wolves are afraid and the call of birds is
drowned,
And the thought and speech of man in the boiling
water's sound.
But upon the further side of the barren, sharp ravine
With the sunlight on its turrets is the castle seen,
Calm and very wonderful, white above the green
Of the wet and waving forest, slanted all away,
Because the driving Northern wind will not rest by
night or day.
Yet the towers are sure above, very mighty is the
stead,
The gates are made of ivory, the roofs of copper red.

Round and round the warders grave walk upon the
walls for ever

And the wakeful dragons couch in the ports of ivory,
Nothing is can trouble it, hate of the gods nor man's
endeavour,
And it shall be a resting-place, dear heart, for you and
me.

Through the wet and waving forest with an age-old
sorrow laden
Singing of the world's regret wanders wild the faerie
maiden,
Through the thistle and the brier, through the tangles
of the thorn,
Till her eyes be dim with weeping and her homeless
feet are torn.
Often to the castle gate up she looks with vain
endeavour,
For her soulless loveliness to the castle winneth never.

But within the sacred court, hidden high upon the
mountain,
Wandering in the castle gardens lovely folk enough
there be,
Breathing in another air, drinking of a purer fountain
And among that folk, beloved, there's a place for you
and me.

DEATH IN BATTLE

Open the gates for me,
Open the gates of the peaceful castle, rosy in the West,
In the sweet dim Isle of Apples over the wide sea's
                                            breast,
Open the gates for me!

Sorely pressed have I been
And driven and hurt beyond bearing this summer day,
But the heat and the pain together suddenly fall away,
All's cool and green.

But a moment agone,
Among men cursing in fight and toiling, blinded I
                                            fought,
But the labour passed on a sudden even as a passing
                                            thought,
And now—alone!

Ah, to be ever alone,
In flowery valleys among the mountains and silent
                                            wastes untrod,
In the dewy upland places, in the garden of God,
This would atone!

I shall not see
The brutal, crowded faces around me, that in their
                                   toil have grown
Into the faces of devils—yea, even as my own—
When I find thee,

O Country of Dreams!
Beyond the tide of the ocean hidden and sunk away,
Out of the sound of battles, near to the end of day,
Full of dim woods and streams.

Notes

1. *Prologue.* (a) Phoenicia was a country forming a narrow strip along the coast of Syria and including Tyre and Sidon. From early times its inhabitants were important as pioneers of navigation and trade. While it is certain that the Greek navigator Pytheus (c. 310–306 B.C.) visited the tin mines of Cornwall and even circumnavigated Britain, the credit for the discovery of the Cornish tin mines has traditionally gone to the Phoenicians. The one who has been thought to have given them the credit is the first great historian, Herodotus. In his very entertaining *History* (Bk. III, chapters 113–114) he says he doesn't 'know anything of the existence of islands called the Tin Islands, whence we get our tin. . . . Yet it cannot be disputed that tin and amber do come to us from what one calls the ends of the earth.'

(b) Baal-Peor and his consort Baalat (the 'horned maiden') were Syrian dieties, the former being one of the heathen gods mentioned in the Old Testament.

(c) 'Brethon treasure' is the British tin taken from the mines in Cornwall.

2. *Victory.* (a) Roland is the hero in Charlemagne's army celebrated in the twelfth-century French epic *The Song of Roland.*

(b) Cuchulain is the most famous hero in Celtic (Irish) mythology.

(c) Helen was, according to Greek legend, the most beautiful woman in the land. The daughter of Zeus and Leda, she was married to Menelaus, king of Sparta. She was abducted by Paris, son of the king of Troy. The *Iliad* of Homer (fl. before 700 B.C.) is the story of the attempt by the Greek princes to recover her from the Trojans.

(d) Iseult was the daughter of the King of Ireland who was married to King Mark of Cornwall. On her way to Cornwall she and Sir Tristram unwittingly drank a love potion, and their love leads to a tragic end.

There are numerous versions of the story, but Lewis was probably thinking of the story as told in Sir Thomas Malory's *Morte Darthur* (1485).

(e) Dryads, in the Greek and Roman myths, were the nymphs of trees. When the trees they inhabited died, they died as well. Naiads were the nymphs of fresh waters and Nereids the nymphs of the Mediterranean Sea.

(f) According to the historian Nennius (fl. 796), in his *Historia Britonum*, Arthur lived in the sixth century as a British *dux bellorum* (military chieftan). He was elevated to King Arthur of the Round Table in *The History of the Kings of Britain* by Geoffrey of Monmouth (1100?-1154). The best-known story of King Arthur is the *Morte Darthur*. After his final battle at Camelford, Arthur is carried to the island of Avalon to be healed of his wounds.

3. *Irish Nocturne.* (a) Grendel is the monster who, in the tenth-century Old English *Beowulf*, kills many of King Hrothgar's thanes at Harte. He is eventually killed by Beowulf.

(b) Balor, who is as evil as Grendel, is the Celtic god of Night.

4. *Apology.* (a) 'Troynovant' is an old spelling for Troy.

(b) Brynhild is the heroine of the thirteenth-century German epic the *Nibelungenlied.* It served as the basis for Richard Wagner's opera *The Ring of the Nibelungs,* composed between 1853-1870.

(c) Maeve is the mortal Queen of Connacht in Celtic mythology.

(d) Bradamant is a maiden warrior in Boiardo's unfinished Italian poem *Orlando Innamorato* (1487). It was completed by Ludovico Ariosto in his *Orlando Furioso* (1532).

5. *The Witch.* The chief sources of the 'winner of the fleece' and the 'Colchian witch' are the *Argonautica* of Apollonius Rhodius (c. 295-215 B.C.) and *Medea,* by Euripides. The *Argonautica* is the story of the voyage of Jason, son of the king of Corinth, and other men on the ship *Argo* to Colchis to recover the Golden Fleece, which had been stolen. Medea, the witch daughter of the king of Colchis, falls in love with Jason

and helps him recover the Fleece. Following their marriage and the birth of three sons, Jason deserts her and marries someone else. The tragic consequences of this become the subject of Euripides' play, in which, because of her savagery, Medea is banished. She contrives the death of Jason's bride and kills her own children in order to make Jason childless, after which she escapes to Athens. She is not killed in the Greek myths, and because of his fascination with the story, Lewis gives Medea a fitting end by having her burnt at the stake in the medieval manner.

6. *The Philosopher.* The 'country where the ancient Mothers dwell' is a reference to Plutarch's *Life of Marcellus* (XX, 2), in which he says, 'There is a city of Sicily called Ergyium, not large, but very ancient, and famous for the appearance there of goddesses, who are called Mothers'. While Plutarch doesn't say who the Mothers are, the Greeks would have probably identified Rhea (the Earth) as one. Rhea was identified by the Asians as Cybele (the 'Great Mother'), who was worshipped under the guise of a block of stone. That stone was brought to Rome in 204 B.C. (Years later Lewis introduced the stone goddess, which he calls Ungit, into his novel *Till We Have Faces.*) However, the terror caused by the 'Mothers' was Goethe's contribution. His source was Plutarch, and in his poem *Faust* he has Mephistopheles say:

> Loath am I now high mystery to unfold:
> Goddesses dwell, in solitude sublime,
> Enthroned beyond the world of space or time.
> Even to speak of them dismays the bold.
> These are The Mothers.

7. *Song of the Pilgrims.* (a) The 'Dwellers at the back of the North Wind' were, according to Greek myths, the Hyperboreans, which word means 'dwellers beyond Boreas' (the North Wind). They worshipped Apollo and lived in a land of perpetual sunshine and plenty. It was George MacDonald who popularised them in his *At the Back of the North Wind* (1871), which Lewis read in May 1916. MacDonald begins this charm-

ing book by saying, 'I do not think Herodotus had got the right account of the place. I am going to tell you how it fared with a boy who went there.' Oddly enough, he found less to say about the Hyperboreans than Herodotus. In his *History,* Herodotus mentions them in a purely historical manner in Book IV, chapter 20, and again in chapter 34, where he ends his account: 'Let me just add . . . that if Hyperboreans exist "beyond the north wind" there must also be Hypernotians "beyond the south." ' The result was that Lewis used his own imagination to describe what lies beyond the North Wind.

(b) The Pilgrims who wander 'from Orkney unto Ind' travel from the Orkney Islands, which lie north of the northernmost tip of Scotland, to 'Ind', which is the Middle English word for India.

(c) The 'Land of the Lotus' refers to the country of Lotus-eaters, a fabulous people who in enticing others to eat the lotus fruit cause them to forget their home and content themselves with remaining forever in Lotus-Land. It comes from Homer's *Odyssey* (Bk. IX).

(d) Herodotus has a great deal to say about 'Scythia', which was the name the Greeks gave to that enormous tract of land between the Carpathian Mountains and the river Don in Russia. The 'Scythian waste' is what we know as the steppes of Russia.

(e) The 'Syrens' were fabulous creatures who had the power of drawing men to destruction by their singing. In the *Odyssey* (Bk. XII) Odysseus saves his men from shipwreck by filling their ears with wax while he has himself lashed to the mast of his ship so he can hear the Syrens.

(f) The 'Pillars' or the 'Pillars of Hercules' are the two mountains, called Calpe (Gibralta) and Abyla, opposite one another at the entrance of the Mediterranean. They were supposed to have been parted by the arm of Hercules.

8. *Ballade Mystique.* 'Dagda' (which means 'The Good') is the supreme head of the People of Dana, in Celtic mythology.

9. *Night.* The 'Country-under-wave' is the island of Atlantis. It means the 'island of Atlas', and it was near the Straits of Gibralta. According to

Greek myth it once ruled southwest Europe and northwest Africa, and it was destroyed when its kings were defeated by the prehistoric Athenians. Although Lewis would have known the story of this underwater country as a child, he first met an historical account of it in Plato, who mentions where and what it was in his dialogues *Critias* and *Timaeus*.

10. *How He Saw Angus the God.* This is Lewis's addition to the Celtic myth of Angus (son of Dagda), the Irish god of Love.

11. *Hesperus.* Although best known as the 'evening star', Hesperus is also the planet Venus.

BOOKS BY C. S. LEWIS
AVAILABLE FROM HARCOURT BRACE & COMPANY
AS A HARVEST PAPERBACK